The Saga of the Déise

by

Leonard Kearon MSc

Illustrations by Leonard Kearon MSc and Joseph Kearon

Printed by Amazon Kindle Direct Publishing

First Printing, 2020

ISBN 9798616311641

For more information email: deisebook@gmail.com

Contents

Introduction

"Up the Déise!" A common cry whenever a Waterford team plays a game. But who or what were the Déise? Who or what were their connection to Waterford City and County. It is surprising that many people don't seem to know. Everyone knows about the Vikings and their connection to Waterford, but the Déise seem to be ignored. Various history books almost treat them as a footnote in Waterford's history.

This is why this book was written, to shine some light on Waterford's ancestors. The men and women who lived in Waterford county, before, during and after the Vikings. From their origins to their rise and fall and all the bits in-between. How they lived their day to day lives, the Gods and God they worshipped, and how they travelled the known world.

I hope you enjoy this book and will have a better knowledge of the Déise, which will be inspired you to discover more about them.

Acknowledgements

The author would like to thank the following people. First my brother Joseph who helped out by drawing some of the images for this book and supporting me through this. Of course, my parents William and Yvonne for their continuous support in this and my other projects. I would like to thank Ian Lennon of TUS and Tom Hosford of St. Patrick's Gateway Centre for giving my first job researching the history of St. Patrick's Gateway Centre and its graveyard. Trish Dolan for convincing me to do this. The staff of Garter Lane Arts Centre for giving me my second job which continued to allow me to do this book and write a history leaflet for them.

I would also like to thank my extended family of uncles, aunts and cousins who kept being interested in the creation of this book and assuring me that I would have a good number of customers when this book would finally be published. I would like to thank the historians of Waterford, past and present, along with the Waterford History Facebook Group and Waterford Treasures Museums for keeping the History of Waterford alive and helping me notice a small gap in the history that I could hopefully help fill.

Finally, I would like to thank you the reader, for reading this book.

Chapter One: The Origin of the Déise

Two thousand years ago, Ireland was a primeval and mystical land. Those who called the island home would have viewed it as sacred, with the landscape and environment having a major impact on their society and culture. At this time, knowledge was passed by learned people through spoken word, but their history can still be read by understanding their landscape, the celestial cycles and with time, writings of ancient scholars. They would have been closely attuned with the mighty mountains, dense forests, beautiful bogs, small areas of fertile land, the ebb and flow of the ocean and the raging rivers. This sacred and varied landscape encouraged, protected and preserved a diverse society in Ireland which still exists to this day. Equally, we can learn about a civilisation by reviewing neighbouring social and political events with which they coincided.

By 116 A.D, the Roman Empire was at the height of its power having conquered most of mainland Europe, Ireland was acknowledged but not understood or conquered. Greek geographer Strabo (64 B.C – 24 A.D), referred to Ireland as being "where the limits of the known world should be placed." Ireland was written about by many ancient European scholars and was known by many different names; Iris by Diodorus Siculus, Iuverna by Pomponius Mela, Ierne by Strabo, Hibernia by Julius Caesar and Iwernia by the Greek geographer Claudius Ptolemy.

Both Diodorus Siculus and Strabo made the claim that the Irish were cannibals, Strabo also suggested that the Irish engaged in incest. Strabo himself was dubious about the credibility of his sources regarding these reports, they would endure for centuries. Later historians such as Geoffrey Keating, refute these unreasonable affiliations and point out that the Irish were a brave and well-educated society whose knowledge and wisdom spread across most of Europe.

Julius Caesar mentioned Ireland in his writings about the Gallic Wars, a military campaign waged against various Celtic tribes across what is now mostly western Europe. He seems to be the first to place Ireland west of Britain, as Strabo placed Ireland, north of Britain and offered no other details. Caesar referred to Ireland as being half the size of Britain and of

being equal distance from Britain, as Britain is to Gaul.

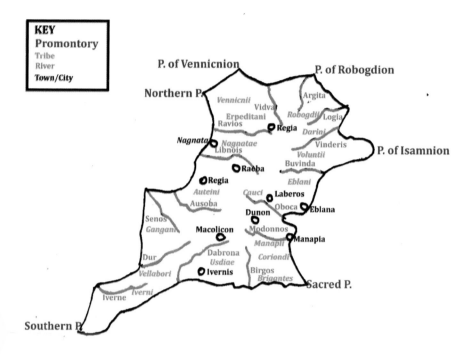

Ptolemy's Map of Ireland

Ptolemy gave us the earliest known map of Ireland which listed

several rivers and tribes including the Menapii. The Menapii, Belgic

seafarers and traders who had sailed their ships around the Irish Sea for

centuries BC, established trading colonies on the Irish, Scottish, Welsh and

Manx coasts. Their first Irish colony, Menapia (216 BC), was established

between present day Waterford and Wexford. Later they settled around

Lough Erne, becoming known as Fir Manach, and giving their name to

Fermanagh and Monaghan. They spread throughout Ireland, evolving into historic Irish clans whose descendants are found worldwide today: Mooney, Meaney, Mannion, Manning, Minogue, Mannix, McMannion, etc.

Claudius Ptolemy

Ptolemy also mentioned a Celtic tribe called the Brigantes who seemed to be based in counties Waterford, Kilkenny and Wexford. They share their name with a Pre-Roman tribe who inhabited what would become most of Northern England. These two tribes, among others mentioned by Ptolemy, suggests that County Waterford was inhabited by European tribes who settled in Ireland after their lands were conquered by the Romans.

Descending from these tribes, were the Déise. The word Déise has had many spellings over the years, Déise, Deis, Decies, Deisí, Degaid, Deesi, Deisigh, among others. For this book we will be using the most common version at this time which is "Déise". The word Déise comes from the Old Irish word 'déis' which translates as 'vassal' or 'subject-people'. A vassal was a person given land by a lord or King in exchange for loyalty. According to

Irish myth, the sons of Mil also known as the Milesians, the common ancestors of all the Irish, brought with them from Iberia a slave called Deise and that is where the word Déise comes from.

Waterford comes from the old Norse word Vadrarjfordr which means either "haven from the windswept sea" or "fjord of the rams". It is no surprise that with both Ireland and the Déise having different names, so did Waterford. The Irish for Waterford is Port Láirge, which means "Larag's port" or "Port/Harbour of the Thigh. There is debate of who or what was Larag, some believe it comes from a Viking called Laraic who is mentioned around 953 A.D. Others believe it comes from the Irish word 'Lárac' which means 'limb' or 'thigh as there is an 11th Century story about a prince whose thigh washed up on the Waterford shore after being lured and killed by sirens. Given that Port Láirge appears in early Irish texts means that the name predates both stories, with many theories on the name's origin including the thigh refers to the shape of Waterford Harbour, which resembles a bent leg, with Waterford City situated on the thigh. In

Pagan times it was also known as "Cuan -Na-Grioth" or "Harbour of the Sun".

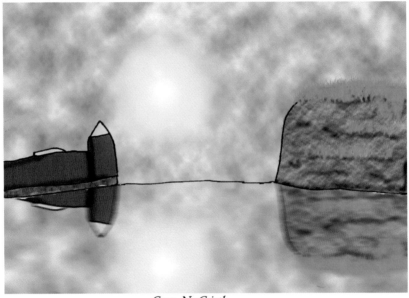

Cuan -Na-Grioth

It was not until the arrival of Christianity that Irish history began to be penned and so the Déise's exact origins are shrouded in the mists of time. There are two main trains of thought on their arrival into Waterford.

The first being that the Déise were the descendants of the people who already lived in the area. At Dunabrattin Head aka Boatstrand near Annestown, County Waterford, there are the remains of a promontory fort, used for protection by the Celtic clan known as the Brattins. A promontory fort was a coastal fort which consisted of fortifications on the landward side. Some believe that the Menapii travelled to Ireland from Iberia and arrived at Dunabrattin. There is also evidence of people settling around Creaden Head near Dunmore East, thousands of years before people like the Brattins and the Menapii. Some believe that the first settlers were, as suggested by Ptolemy's map, various tribes who settled in Ireland after their lands were conquered by the Romans. Others even believe that the Irish came from as far as Greece or Scythia, a kingdom that thrived around both the Black and Caspian Seas.

The second is The Expulsion of the Déise, to date our only written account of the Déise's origin. However, since the first known version of this story dates back to the 8th Century, roughly 500 years after the events of the story, it is hard to determine how much of the story is true and how much is the creation of an 8th Century scholars trying to romanticise their origins.

The Expulsion of the Déise took place at the end of Cormac Mac Airt's reign as King of Tara, which was somewhere around 258 A.D. – 267 A.D. At this time, the Crisis of the Third Century was in full swing in mainland Europe. This was a period where the Roman Empire was on the verge of collapse due to constant invasions, civil wars, plagues and economic problems. Gallienus was Emperor of Rome, having been made Emperor in 253 A.D. and reigning until 268 A.D. This is also believed to be the time of Fionn mac Cumhaill and the Fianna.

As it is the only written record of the Déise's origin we will now tell the story of The Expulsion of the Déise.

The Expulsion of the Déise.

The story of the Déise started in Co. Meath near Tara, where the

clan Déise had large areas of land and were led by four brothers, Brecc, Eochaid, Forad and Óengus. Óengus was known as Óengus of the dread Spear for it is claimed he held the Lúin Celtchair, the legendary Spear of the God Lugh. According to legend, the Lúin Celtchair was a long fiery spear that had to be

Óengus

contained in a cauldron of red fluid in order to prevent it igniting and killing the user. It also was restrained by three chains, each requiring a number of strong warriors to hold it.

The king of Tara at the time was Cormac mac Airt who ruled Tara for forty years. Cormac had three sons, Dáire, Cellach and Cairbre Lifecahir. During this time, Forad's daughter; Forach was kidnapped by Cellach. Óengus learned of what happened and demanded that Cellach release his niece. Cellach refused and took Forach to Tara where he sought the protection of his father.

Cormac mac Airt

Cellach kidnaps Forach

Óengus and his brothers raised a small army and marched on Tara. Once they arrived in the great hall, they demanded Forach be released, but Cellach again refused. Enraged Óengus threw the Lúin Celtchair at Cellach. Cellach was killed instantly and one of Cormac's advisors was wounded.

However, one of the spear's chains struck Cormac and blinded him in one eye. Cormac was forced to abdicate, as according to Irish law, a King had to be without blemishes. Some historians say that Cormac wore a mind, which was a kind of

Forach is Freed

headwear, made of 24 small leaves of red gold, furnished with springs and rollers of white silver that disguised his damaged eye, as to defeat the Déise before abdicating.

With Forach freed and angry at her mistreatment, the Déise demanded independence from Tara and many of them rose up in rebellion. Cormac, wanting to avenge his son's death and being forced to give up his throne, raised an army with his son Cairbre Lifecahir (who would succeed him as King) to crush the Déise. After seven battles, the Déise were defeated and all those who rebelled were exiled from Tara. The Déise that remained loyal to Cormac were called the North Déise, while the exiled Déise became known as the South Déise.

17

With no home, the Déise headed south towards the lands of Uí Bairrche, which is believed to be around County Laois. There the Déise make an alliance with the local ruler Fiachu Bacceda and drove the kin-based group the Uí Bairrche from their lands. The Déise stayed there for about thirty years before the Uí Bairrche regrouped and reclaimed their territories.

Homeless again, the Déise headed further south arriving in Ard Ladrann, near present day Gorey, County Wexford. The Déise were given land by Crimthann mac Énnai, the King of Leinster who later married various daughters of the Déise leaders.

One of his daughters from these marriages was Ethne the Dread, who was prophesised to help her mother's people find their homeland. She was

Ethne the Dread

known as Ethne the Dread as upon learning of the prophecy, her parents fed her young boys to force her to grow faster.

Around the same time, the king of Tara tried to persuade the Déise back to Tara, he offered the sons of Brecc, twice as much land as they had before and guaranteed them peace and forgiveness. Óengus convinced them to reject his offer and stay with their people by promising them that their sons will become the Kings of the Déise. Meanwhile, Eochaid and his family travelled across the Irish Sea and arrived in Wales. We will learn more about the Déise and the Welsh Connection in a later chapter.

The new arrangement in Leinster was not to last, as when Crimthann died, his sons turned on the Déise and their sister, exiling them from the Kingdom of Leinster. The Déise attempted to live in the Kingdom of Osraige, now County Kilkenny; but the King of Osraige destroyed their homes and drove them into the Kingdom of Munster.

Óengus mac Nad Froích, the King of Munster had fallen in love with Ethne and wanted to marry her. To woo her, he promised to grant her three wishes as her dowry. Ethne agreed to his proposal in exchange for the Déise to be given land therefore fulfilling her prophecy, revenge on the Kingdom of Osraige by exiling them and their territory to be given to the Déise, and finally for the Déise to be declared a free people.

The King of Munster granted his new wife her three wishes; but the Déise had problems defeating the people of Osraige. They fought seven battles but failed to make any significant gains. Ethne told them to seek the Druids' help and the Druids revealed an ancient prophecy that whoever was first to spill blood on the next day of battle would be exiled. With this knowledge the Déise druids transformed a soldier into a Red Cow. When the Osraige army saw the cow the next morning, they killed it and since they split blood first, they were exiled.

With the defeat of the Osraige, and the King of Munster's promise, the Déise had found a new home. For a time, the Déise had land that included parts of County Limerick and even as far as Cashel in County Tipperary. However more often, the Déise's home was a land that stretched North to the Suir and South to the sea, to Lismore in the West and Creaden Head in the East, which forms what is largely now County Waterford.

Chapter 2: Life of the Déise

Having found a permanent home, the Déise began to settle all over their land. Their abodes were generally ringforts, circular fortified settlements, which consisted of; a round house roughly six to seven metres in diameter, dwellings for animals and buildings to store and make food and tools in. Constructions were built using any available composite materials. Wattle and daub, a method of filling a wooden frame with a sticky material of mud, dung and straw, or stone was common. The roundhouse could be expanded by adding rectangular rooms to the outside or a second roundhouse could be built and linked to the original, creating a figure of eight.

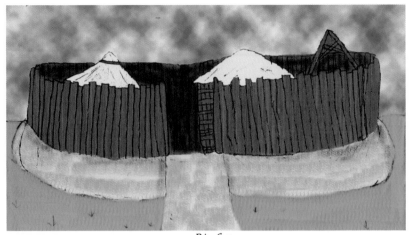

Ringfort

The ringfort was sometimes raised and generally surrounded by a wooden fence and ditch with an entranceway cutting across at one point that led to a gate. Some ringforts were surrounded by water and built on an artificial island of local materials; these were called Crannógs. Many ringforts had a souterrain, an underground passage, which was used to store items, in times of attack souterrains could be used as a hiding place or an escape route. As the economy was largely agricultural, with cows and slaves being used as currency, the size and complexity of a ringfort was a symbol of a person's status along with the clothes they wore.

Déise Man and Woman

Lower classes wore a jacket with tight trousers of various lengths.
The aristocracy wore a voluminous cloak called a brat over a linen shirt or
tunic called a léine. The brat was secured by a brooch. The amount of
colour a person wore was also a status symbol, although it is believed this
code only occurred at times of public meetings. Slaves were only allowed to
wear clothes of one colour while farmers wore two colours. The colour scale
continued until six, which was the amount of colour Royalty could wear.
Beards and Moustaches were popular with men, though generally beards
were reserved for upper classes and generally forked. For warriors, their

moustaches and hair were braided into a style known as a glib, which offered some protection and allowed the concealment of weapons. For non-warriors and women, the hair was left to grow long.

The Déise were a Pagan society with many Gods and ethical codes by which they lived their day to day life. They had their own Pantheon, the Tuatha Dé Danann, which means the Tribe of the Goddess Dana. Their beliefs were largely based on the natural world with the landscape and the celestial cycles shaping their religion. Due to the amount of information on Paganism we will discuss it further in a future chapter.

The Brehon Laws were the ethical code used by the Déise. Sculpted to perfection over hundreds of years and passed down orally from generation to generation when finally, they were written down in 7th Century AD, these laws formed the Déise's legal system. By studying the Déise's jurisprudence, or philosophy of their law, we can assume the mindset of these intermittently progressive people.

The law was administered by the Brehons, learned men and women who acted as judge and arbitrator and where highly respected as there was no police force or court system during this time. The laws were based around the idea of restitution not punishment, in fact there were no prisons and no capital punishment. Most cases were resolved by the offender paying the victim a fine. Naturally the size of the fine depended on the severity of the crime, even being guilty of murder resulted in the payment of a fine. There were punishments for not paying a fine such as loss of status, exile and in extreme circumstances the offender could become the property of the victim or his family who could do as they pleased with him.

The laws treated both genders equally, in a divorce for example, only the assets procured during the marriage were divided, any assets either person had before the marriage remained the property of that person. The

Brehon with a Sín

Brehons and the law were so respected in the country, that few would contemplate taking the law into their own hands. Instead they believed that through the Brehons and their judgements, justice would be done. To prove

their judgements were true and correct, some Brehons like legendary
Morann wore a special collar called a sín which tightened around their neck
if they delivered a false judgement and who expanded if they delivered a
truthful judgement.

As mentioned previously, the Brehon Laws were written down
during the 7th Century. Two of the most important law books to be
written were the Senchas Mór and the Book of Aicill. The Senchas Mór was
a large book which detailed all the laws of Ireland at the time of Saint
Patrick. The book was commissioned by Saint Patrick, who wanted to have
a written record, however any laws that would contradict Christian doctrine
would have been either removed or edited. The Book of Aicill mostly dealt
with criminal law. According to legend, this book was written by Cormac
Mac Airt, after he retired to Aicill, now the Hill of Skreen, after he was
forced to abdicate following the loss of his eye to Óengus.

Despite the arrival of the Vikings, the Normans and the English,
the Brehon Laws survived outside the Pale. Despite various attempts, the
Brehon Laws continued to be the Deise man's long-standing opus with
various settlers preferring to employ them over their own laws. The Brehon

Laws were eventually supplanted by English Common Law in the 17th Century.

The Brehon Laws also formed the basis for the Déise's system of Government. There was no central government at the time, instead Ireland was divided into over 150 small kingdoms each called a Tuatha and ruled by their own king or chieftain. The King of the Déise was generally a member of the O'Faoláin family, they lived at Rathmoylan, Lisselan and Ballinanessagh. The Prince of the Déise was generally a member of the O'Bric family who were cousins of the O'Faoláins, and they lived in Ballybricken. Other prominent Déise families included; O'Mera, O'Meara, O'Flanagan, O'Breslin, O'Foley and O'Keane.

All the families were required to pay a tribute to their King, the King of Déise received 8 slaves, 8 horses, a full rigged ship, 8 shields, 8 swords and 8 lances. In turn each King would have to pay a tribute to the King of their Province. The Déise's tribute to the King of Munster included 1,000 oxen, 1,000 sheep, 1,000 cows that have calved and 1,000 cloaks with white borders. In return the King of Munster would give the King of the Déise; 8 horses, 8 green cloaks and 8 brooches made of Findruine

(White Bronze). Paying the tribute was important as it gave the person, the King's protection and a voice in the King's court.

While most of Mainland Europe had benefited from a vast network of Roman Roads, Ireland had its own road network. It was quite basic, linking Tara with the rest of the country, with each road being called a Slige. A Slige was a track which was wide enough for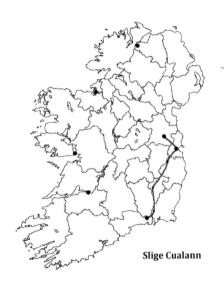

Slige Cualann

two chariots to pass each while going at speed. The Slige Cualann was the slige which linked Waterford to Dublin and Tara and passed through Dunlavin, Leighlinbridge and New Ross. Smaller roads were mostly used by people on foot or on horseback.

One of the earliest roads in the Déise was Rian Bó Pádraig – "The track of Patrick's Cow". It linked Ardmore and Cashel and was supposed to have been created by one of Saint Patrick's cows wandering from Cashel to Ardmore. The road is mentioned in the Life of Saint Declan who made many trips from his home in Ardmore to Cashel, where the King of Munster lived. As Ireland has many rivers and lakes, boats were also used. These boats were called naomhógs by the Déise and other Munster people, or currachs by other Irish people and were made of either wood or animal hides and some could even sail across seas. These boats allowed the Déise to travel to Britain and mainland Europe, spreading their knowledge, trading goods and capturing slaves.

In society, slaves were part of the Daor Aicme class or Unfree, along with prisoners and their descendants. They had no land of their own but could be given some of the poorest ground. While they were owned by a person or a tribe, Daor Aicme still had some protection under the law. As in many cultures, it was possible for a Daor Aicme, to gain his freedom and move through the ranks of society to become a true member of the tribe.

Above the Daor Aicme, there was the Saor Aicme or the free. This class was largely made up of people who owned land and animals. They had to pay a rent to the tribe, which was used for the benefit of the whole tribe, not the landlord. The Daor Aicme were also warriors and were required to fight when called upon.

Ranking higher again were the Aos Dána or the Professionals, consisting of the Brehons, Poets, Historians, Druids and Musicians. Chieftains and kings made sure they had a few Aos Dana in their employ at all times. They too had tremendous power and wealth and could sometimes be even more affluent and distinguished than chieftains themselves.

The Déise diet was based on whatever the land gave them. Their food mostly consisted of bread, honey, pork, butter, venison and apples. While they had cattle and sheep, they were kept to produce milk and wool rather than for food. Déise Drinks included milk, mead and a beer called coirm.

The Déise like the rest of the country spoke Irish. The earliest written version of Irish survives on the numerous Ogham stones that are scattered around County Waterford and the rest of Munster. These series of lines formed the first Irish alphabet. By the 7th Century, Irish was being written in the Roman alphabet and the various invaders and settlers learned and even added to it.

As shown a large portion of the Déise's culture survived the numerous invasions that threatened the land. The invaders seemed to have taken a shine to the Irish culture and decided to settle here for that reason. Despite being known for their pillaging and violence, the Vikings and the Déise coexisted together, with both sides working together to repel other invaders. It is theorised that the Vikings and the Déise could have made a deal which led to the creation of Waterford City.

While we have explored the life of the Déise, we did only glance at one of the most important parts of their lives, which we will go into more in detail next: Religion.

Chapter 3: Religion

The Déise like the rest of Ireland and the known world started as a Pagan society. As Ireland wasn't conquered by the Romans, the Irish religion wasn't destroyed by or assimilated into the Roman religion. As Ireland was known but not understood during Roman times, there were many claims about their beliefs by ancient scholars. Many ancient scholars claimed the Irish practiced human sacrifices while Julius Caesar claiming the use of Wicker Men but there is little evidence for any of these claims.

Unlike many religions of the time, there were no temples or churches instead open-air altars and sacred sites formed the meeting point for worship and festivals. Tory Hill in County Kilkenny, for example, was the site of festivals and games dedicated to the God Lugh. Idols were also worshipped around the country with the Cromm Cruach idol in County Cavan being the most famous.

There was an idol in Clonea, near Dungarvan which had sunken eyes, a hideous face and a depression in its head for offerings. According to local legend, a sailor from Clonea took the idol from its resting place and placed it above his bed in his cabin. He started to

The Hideous Idol of Clonea

get sick and was told by a priest that unless he buried the idol he had stolen, he would die. The sailor buried the idol at sea and was cured. Months later, he returned to Clonea after his voyage and visited the ruined priory. To his horror, in the corner on a stone slab, was the same idol he had buried at sea.

The Cloch Labhrais

While not an idol, the Cloch Labhrais or Speaking Stone, north of

Durrow, County Waterford was said to have magical powers, being able to

speak and tell if someone was telling the truth. The stone has a large crack

which splits it in half. According to local legend, a woman was accused of

cheating on her husband, but she denied it. The husband planned to bring

her to the Cloch Labhrais to see if she was telling the truth. Before her

"trial", the woman arranged for her lover to stand on a hill close to the rock

where he could be seen but not close enough to be recognised. When she

was brought to the Cloch Labhrais, she pointed to the man on the hill, her

lover, and proclaimed she had no more to do with the man accused by her

husband as she did with the man over on the hill. When the husband asked

the Cloch Labhrais if this was true, the Cloch Labhrais replied it was true,

but the truth is often bitter. Disgusted with the woman's evil in manipulating the truth, the Cloch Labhrais split in two and never spoke again.

Sacred Tree Leaves

Like everything else in their lives, the Irish religion was based on nature, the elements and the celestial cycles. Certain trees including; oak, hazel, hawthorn, rowan, ash and elder were deemed sacred and were believed to have magical powers. Oak was seen to have healing properties, sexual powers and aid in decision making. Since it was the sacred tree of the Dadga, Oak was used to make staffs for Kings to help them make wise decisions during their reign. Hazel was believed to be the Tree of Knowledge; hawthorn was believed to be used by fairies as a meeting place and could bring good luck to the owner. Rowan could prevent the dead rising again and negate evil spells. Ash was known as the Tree of

Enchantment and was used to mark sacred sites. Druids made their staffs out of ash, so they could use their magic. Elder was considered an evil and cursed tree, used by witches and a favourite of fairies, though it also had healing properties if the correct prayers and spells were used.

Ireland was said to have five sacred trees were seen as the mystical guardians of the island. They were the Eo Mughna an oak or yew tree located at Ballaghmoon in County Kildare. The Bile Tortan was an ash tree located near Navan in County Meath, the Eo Ruis a yew tree in Old Leighlin in County Carlow, the Craeb Daithi, another ash this time in Farbill in County Westmeath and the Craeb Uisnig was also an ash, located in Uisneach, County Westmeath.

Many clans had their own sacred tree called a bile. These trees marked the inauguration site of Kings and were important in the inauguration ceremony. As well as being a sacred tree, the bile could also refer to a sacred grove. Given the spiritual and political important of these trees, they were a common target in battles against warring tribes. The bile belonging to Brian Boru's tribe at Magh Adhair in County Clare is recorded to have been attack twice in the annals.

Elemental worship was common in Ireland, though there doesn't seem to be a universal system for worship. Instead, what elements were worshipped and how, depended on the location or even individual. Water, Fire and the Sun seem to the most common elements to worship.

Water worship was common around wells, which some believed druids were buried under and wells were often associated with having healing powers. The Sun was worshiped everywhere and many of the Irish Gods were Sun Gods, as it was very common, Saint Patrick is said to have warned the Irish that adoring the Sun would lead to eternal death. Fire was worshiped by the Druids, who lit bonfires during various festivals. The elements were so important and revered that swearing an oath on the elements was common. In 461 AD a king swore by the "sun and moon, water and air, day and night, sea and land" he would not enforce a tribute, only to break his oath two years later and according to reports "the sun and wind killed him because he had violated them."

As well as the sun, the celestial cycles; the movement of the stars, were worshipped. Around the country, tombs, standing stones and idols were built to align with the various celestial cycles. The summer and winter solstices; the longest and shortest days of the year, were of significant importance as many monuments were designed to tap into the mystical and

spiritual energies of these events. Newgrange is the most famous example of celestial alignment in Ireland, but there are local examples; the Knockeen

Knockeen Dolmen

Dolmen outside Waterford City seems to align with the setting sun of the Summer Solstice, while the Knockroe Passage Tomb in County Kilkenny is aligned to the rising and setting sun of the Winter Solstice.

In Pagan religion, the main spiritual leaders were the Druids. Druids were known as the wisest people in the land and were knowledgeable in all fields including law, history and medicine. The druids were part of Aos Dána or the Professional class and were the most influential and powerful, acting as advisors and counsellors to kings and being allowed to educate a king's children. As with other professions like the Brehons, women could also become druids and were called druidesses.

The druids were powerful magicians, who could use their magic as they saw fit. In some stories, it was the strength of the druid not the army that won battles. Thanks to their powers, the druids were respected and sometimes feared as they were known to curse people and clans with bouts of madness or forgetfulness. They could foresee

A Druidess

future events by studying natural occurrences, communicating with certain birds or performing various rites and incantations. Druids could create a Fe-fiada, which could render a person or object invisible, and many of the entrances to the Otherworld and fairy forts had a Fe-fiada surrounding them.

The coming of Christianity had mixed fortunes for the druids in Ireland. With a new religion dominating the land, a lot of their duties were now being done by bishops and priests, so their importance began to diminish. However, a lot of their knowledge could now be written down, allowing for it to be preserved and passed on to future generations.

Like many Polytheistic religions such as the Romans, Greeks and Norsemen, the Irish had their own Pantheon called the Tuatha Dé Danann, which means the Tribe of the Goddess Dana. According to their beliefs, the Tuatha Dé Danann lived in the Otherworld, a mystical land full of everlasting youth, health and joy. The Otherworld is called by many names in Irish myths including Tír nAill and Tír na nÓg. According to legend, the Otherworld could be accessed by entering burial mounds like Brú na Bóinne or diving into certain lakes or crossing the Western Ocean.

A Fomorian

The Tuatha Dé Danann battled the Fomorians, a race of violent Gods who lived on Tory Island, off the coast of Donegal. The Fomorians were generally described as being monstrous, sometimes they are described as having only one eye, arm and leg, other sources claim they were goat-headed humanoids. However, some Fomorians like Elatha were described as being very handsome.

Though the relationship between the two races is complex due to some Tuatha Dé Danann and Fomorians marrying each other in an attempt to forge peace. Lugh, one of the Tuatha Dé Danann greatest heroes was part Fomorian from his mother Ethniu. On the other hand, Bres who was the son of Elatha of the Fomorians and Ériu, was a tyrant who sided with his father's people and enslaved his mother's people. The relationship of the two races was similar to that of the Aesir and Jötnar of Norse mythology.

The Fomorians were
defeated by the Tuatha Dé Danann
at the Second Battle of Mag Tuired,
in County Sligo. The battle saw the
Tuatha Dé Danann rise up against
Bres who enlisted the help of Balor of
the Poisonous Eye, a Fomorian King
and giant with the ability to kill

Balor

anything by looking at it. The battle ended when Lugh
killed Balor, who was his grandfather, with a sling or spear and Balor's eye
was still open and shone on the Fomorian army. The poisonous eye killed
most of the Fomorians and created Loch na Súil in County Sligo. Bres was
spared by Lugh when Bres promised to teach the Tuatha Dé Danann about
farming.

Below are some of the Tuatha Dé Danann:

The Dadga: King of the Tuatha Dé Danann, though unlike other
Pantheons, he wasn't seen as a supreme God like Zeus or Odin, as he came

from a line of kings. He was the God of fertility, farming, manliness and wisdom. He was armed with the Lorg Mór, a club which could kill with one end and resurrect people with the handle. He also had the Uaithne, a harp which could affect emotions and the seasons. Like many King of the Gods from other Pantheons, the Dadga mated with many women and fathered many children.

Danu: The mother goddess of the Tuatha Dé Danann and who the Pantheon is named after. She was worshipped as a goddess of plenty and had a strong following in Munster. She is commemorated by the Paps of Anu near Killarney in County Kerry,

Clíodhna: The Queen of the Banshees and is associated with various important families in Munster, especially in Cork. She is also seen as a goddess of love, given some of her myths involves her either waiting her lover or chasing after suitors. She is also credited with creating the Blarney Stone. Her palace was said to be Carrig-Cleena, outside Mallow in County Cork.

Lugh: The Tuatha Dé Danann's greatest hero and the God of skills, crafts and the arts. He is known for being a master of all skills as well as being a sky god. He wielded many artefacts including the Lúin Celtchair. He was part Fomorian as his mother was Ethniu, the daughter of the Fomorian leader Balor of the poisonous eye. Lugh later killed Balor when the

Lugh

Fomorians attempted to invade the Otherworld. The harvest festival Lughnasadh, which happened on the last Sunday of July or first Sunday in August, celebrated his victory over the evil Crom Dubh. Lúnasa, the Irish for August is also named after him.

The Morrigan: A trio of warrior goddess, consisting of Badb, Macha and either Nemain or Anand. The Morrigan is sometimes referred to as a singular entity and may have been another wife or at least a lover of the Dadga. The Morrigan plays a similar role to the Valkyries of Norse myth, foretelling death on the Battlefield, generally appearing in the form of a Crow. A common belief for a warrior was that if they saw the Morrigan washing their armour and weapons, then that warrior would die in their next battle They appear in a couple of Cú Chulainn's stories as both an ally or an enemy, including his death and aided Lugh in a couple of stories as well.

Ler: The God of the Sea, though he is often overshadowed by his son Manannán mac Lir, who succeed him as God of the Sea and Guardian of the Otherworld. It is believed that Ler is also the king, or the inspiration for the king, mentioned in the Irish myth The Children of Lir. Manannán mac Lir was also worshipped on the Isle of Man, which is named after him and in Wales.

Brigid: The daughter of the Dadga and Goddess of healing, fertility, craft, poetry and Spring. She is seen to have some similarities with Hestia, the Greek Goddess of home and family. Brigid's feast day was Imbolc, which celebrated the start of Spring. Given her name and feast day, many believe she was combined with the Christian Saint Brigid or even Saint Brigid is the Christianization of the Tuatha Dé Danann goddess.

Ogma: The God of language and learning and son of the Dadga. He is known for his friendly rivalry with Lugh and being one of the Tuatha Dé Danann's champions. He apparently dies in battle with the Fomorian King, Indech, though some accounts suggest he survived. It is said that he invented the Ogham alphabet, which we will learn about later in this book.

Banba, Ériu and Fódla: An important trio of Goddess sisters, who each wanted to give their name to Ireland with Banba being credited as being the first person to set foot in Ireland, though other legends say it was Cesaire. According to legend, the three sisters each asked the bard Amergin to name the Island after her. Given that Ireland is also called Érin or Éire it seems that Ériu won, but the bard also allowed both Banba and Fódla to be used as names for Ireland in literature. Another version of the legend says that the three sisters were asked to predict the future of the Tuatha Dé Danann. Ériu gave the most accurate prediction and therefore the island was named after her.

The Tuatha Dé Danann were not the first settlers in Ireland, in fact they were the fifth. The first settlers were led by Cesaire, a woman who built her own ark to survive the Great Flood. She along with her followers landed on the Dingle Peninsula in County Kerry. Sadly, as the group had fifty women and three men, the race eventually died out. Cesaire's husband, Fintan survived due to magic and lived for five thousand years guiding the people of Ireland. Approximately three hundred years later, the second settlers arrived led by Partholon, a Greek giant who was trying to escape a curse put upon him for killing his parents. He arrived near Kenmare in County Kerry, and soon he and his followers were the first to battle the Fomorians at the Battle of Mag Itha, the first ever battle on Irish soil. The Partholonians were victorious and they expanded the landscape creating new waterways and plains. The Partholonians were prosperous for many years but the Fomorians got their revenge, unleashing a plague which killed every single Partholonians in one week.

Thirty years later, the powerful druid Nemed and his family arrived in Ireland. On their way to Ireland, Nemed and his fleet of thirty-two boats saw a tower made of gold in the sea. They attempted to seize the tower, but the sea rose up in anger and destroy all but one ship and killed nine hundred and fifty-one Nemedians. As with the Partholonians before them, the Nemedians battled the Fomorians after three epic battles, the Nemedians were victorious. The Nemedians expanded the land, creating more lakes and plains, however Nemed never got the tower of gold out of his mind. He

forced the Fomorians' greatest craftsmen to build him a better tower. When

the tower was finished, Nemed killed the craftsmen to make sure they could

never build a tower like his again.

The Fomorians attacked the Nemedians in revenge and managed to

defeat them. The Fomorians forced a massive tribute on the Nemedians of

one-third of everything the Nemedians produced including children. The

Nemedians in time built up their forces and attacked Tory Island, the home

of the Fomorians. They managed to seize the Fomorians main tower, but

the Fomorians used their powerful water magic to make the sea drown

nearly all the Nemedians barring two small groups. They were then

banished from Ireland, with one group heading North and the other group

headed East.

The Eastern group eventually arrived in the Mediterranean where

they were captured and made into slaves. They became known as the Fir

Bolg or men of the sacks as they were forced to carry heavy loads for their

masters. Eventually after many generations, they managed to escape and

returned to Ireland. With the help of Fintan, the Fir Bolg defeated the

Fomorians and took back the land of their ancestors. Learning from their ancestors' mistakes, they divided the country into four provinces each having its own ruler and a fifth area at Tara where the High King would rule from and get council from the wisest men in the land.

The Fir Bolg's reign in Ireland lasted only thirty-seven years before the next settlers arrived; the Tuatha Dé Danann. The Tuatha Dé Danann were descended from the Nemedians who had travelled North. They had prospered following their exile unlike their cousins and had gained magically powers and wisdom. Realising they shared a common ancestor, the two tried to live in peace by dividing the country equally, but the Fir Bolg had become a proud warrior race and wanted to fight. In the first Battle of Mag Tuired, the Tuatha Dé Danann won but their leader Nuada was injured and couldn't rule. This led to Bres ruling and enslaving the Tuatha Dé Danann.

The Tuatha Dé Danann thrived for many generations until a High King died and his three sons argued over who should succeed him. In an attempt to prevent a civil war, they asked a wanderer called Ith, what they should do. Ith, who had come from Spain, suggested the three brothers consult the law. They agreed and thanked Ith for his help. Ith travelled

Ireland praising it. The Tuatha Dé Danann began to believe that Ith's praising meant he was planning to conquer Ireland, so they killed him. News of Ith's unprovoked murder reached his son Mil, back in Spain. Mil gathered his sons and set sail to Ireland to get his revenge. Mil died on the voyage, but his sons vowed to honour their father's wish. The Milesians arrived in Ireland and used their druids to combat the Tuatha Dé Danann's magic. On the Plains of Tailtiu in County Meath, the two armies clashed. The Tuatha Dé Danann were defeated and driven from the land, taking refuge in the Otherworld. The Milesians became the ancestors of all Irish people.

Fairies were also worshipped and in particular the side or shee, a group of Earth-Gods who were intertwined with the Tuatha Dé Danann. They lived underneath various fairy-forts which formed the hills and mounts of Ireland. Each elf-fort had a Fe-fiada around it to hide the inhabitants from mortal eyes. During Samhain or Halloween, the Fe-fiada would disappear and mortals could risk seeing inside.

However, many didn't risk it as all supernatural entities including Leprecháns, Goblins also known as Pookas, War-Goblins and Elves ran rampant that night. Fairies were often feared as they were known to use their magic to harm people more than help them.

Fairy, Leprechán and Pooka

Offerings and prayers were used to keep on the fairies' good side as angering them could lead to crops, farm animals and livelihoods being destroyed. Even to this day, people are reluctant to disturb fairy-forts for fear of misfortunate being brought upon them.

As with all religions, burying and respecting the dead was important to the Déise. Many were buried in cists, small stone-lined graves covered with a capstone. These cists sometimes had mounds of earth covering them and may have had ditch. Originally the bodies were cremated but even before the arrival of Christianity, people were being buried intact. As today, these cists could be located together in a cemetery. Monuments like Dolmens, passage tombs, etc, weren't as common when the Déise were around and were sometimes used as sacred sites.

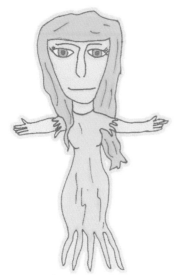
The Banshee

With regards to the dead and beliefs, it is worth noting the Banshee. The Banshee was a fairy who appeared as a young woman, a middle-aged woman or an old hag dressed in a grey robe or dress. The Banshee foretold someone's death usually by a terrifying mourning wail, but other signs of imminent death included seeing her washing the blood-stained clothes of the soon to be deceased or even encountering her. Even to this day, people claim to hear the wail of the Banshee.

The Déise seemed to have different beliefs regard what happened to them after they died. Reincarnation was one, where a person's soul was transformed and reborn each time. A common occurrence with reincarnation seems to be that a soul takes on the form of various animals before being reincarnated as a human. According to various stories, it was possible for a person to retain all the memories and skills of their past lives.

The Déise believed in an afterlife but there is very little information at this time about it. According to some beliefs, the dead would travel west towards Tech Duinn, 'The House of Donn'. Donn was the God of the Dead, but he wasn't part of the Tuatha Dé Danann, he was a Milesian. Tech Duinn is believed to be Bull Rock off the southwest coast of Ireland, known for its dolmen-like shape. According to legend, when a soul arrived at Tech Duinn, it could remain there or find way to the Otherworld or get reincarnated.

Some believed that when they died, their soul would go into one of the many hills and enter the Otherworld. There the soul would live with the fairies and the Tuatha Dé Danann and remain forever young and live in happiness. Many believed that you had to be invited by the Gods of the fairies to enter the Otherworld. Some maps show a mysterious island of the west coast of Ireland called Hy-Brasil, which some believed was the Island of the Dead and could only be visible every seven years.

Whatever the belief, unlike Christianity or many other religions, the Irish Pagan religion makes no mention of a place for the soul of evil people. There is no mention of anything like Hell, Tartarus or Hel and there seems to be no punishment for the souls of evil people. Apparently, they were treated like every other soul, though it is unlikely they would be invited to the Otherworld.

Eventually Christianity began to spread across the land and soon the Pagan religion began to decline. The Tuatha Dé Danann were no longer worshipped as Gods but weren't forgotten as many of their stories were rewritten by scholars to form Ireland's history with the Tuatha Dé Danann being portrayed as mystical kings and queens instead of being Gods. Pagan festivals were transformed in Christian festivals, the festival of Lughnasadh was turned into a festival celebrating Christianity's victory over Paganism and is still celebrated to this day. Christian churches were built near sacred Pagan sites to attract possible converts, there are the ruins of a church very close to the Knockeen Dolmen, for example. While Saint Patrick is credited with converting the Irish to Christianity, in the lands of the Déise, another man was already converting them to the new religion, Saint Declan.

Chapter 4: St Declan: Patron Saint of the Déise

In 312-313 A.D, the Roman Emperor Constantine converted to Christianity allowing what was originally a Middle Eastern cult to spread across the Roman Empire without fear of persecution. Eventually Christianity reached Ireland and in 432 A.D. St Patrick began his mission to convert the Pagan Irish to Christianity. However, there were Christians in Ireland before Saint Patrick's arrival, Saint Palladius was sent to Ireland in 431 A.D. by Pope Celestine I to become the first Bishop of the Christians in Ireland. Meanwhile in the land of the Déise, Saint Declan was converting his people to the new Christian faith.

Saint Declan was born in the late 4th Century in Drumroe, East of

Cappoquin, County Waterford. His parents were Eirc or Ere Mac Trein

and his wife Deithin, and he was a descendant of Eochaid, one of the four

brothers that led the Déise during their

expulsion. According to his Life, when

he was born a fireball flew from his

house creating a ladder accompanied

by angels. This was a sign that Declan

was to become a great and important

Christian. With his parent's blessing

Declan was raised and taught by

Colman, a local priest and later by

another priest called Dioma.

Saint Declan

After many years, Declan

travelled to Rome to continue his studies. It was in Rome he befriended a

bishop called Ailbe, who would later become the Patron Saint of Munster.

In time, Declan was made a bishop and headed back to Ireland. On his way

home, he encountered the future Saint Patrick who was travelling to Rome

to become a bishop. The two became friends and eventually continued their journeys, confident they would meet again. As he continued his journey home, Declan was giving Mass at a church when a small black bell descended from Heaven, this bell would become Saint Declan's most prized and famous relic. Declan entrusted the bell to a follower called Runan to hold and protect it.

Declan arrived back in Ireland and was reunited with Ailbe, along with two more bishops, Ibar, who would become the Patron Saint of Wexford and Ciarán, who would become the Patron Saint of Ossory. The four bishops began their mission to convert the people of Ireland, starting with their own people. With that, Declan headed towards the land of the Déise. Upon arriving back home, Declan began to convert his fellow Déise and quickly gathered several followers. He soon had trouble with the King of Cashel, Aongus MacNatfrich, while Aongus had no problem with Declan preaching and converting in his Kingdom, he refused to convert as he had a rivalry with the Déise, and Declan was of Déise nobility.

Declan made a couple of trips to Rome; it is said on one trip that he befriended Saint David but given the supposed dates of the Saints it seems unlikely. Returning home from another trip, Runan briefly left the bell in the care of another follower, who left it on a rock at the shore.

Declan and his followers were about halfway through their voyage, when

they discovered the bell was missing. Devastated Declan prayed to God to

bring him back his bell and the bell along with the rock appeared before the

boat. The rock continued to travel ahead of the boat and Declan ordered his

disciples to follow it. Eventually the rock and bell led them to a small island

off the Waterford coast called Aird na gCcaorac or High Sheep Island as it

was covered with sheep that belonged to the wife of the King of the Déise.

His disciples were confused as the little hilly island didn't seem big enough

to support them, but Declan told them not to call it a little hill but instead

refer it to as a great height or "Ard Mór." He then proceeded to ask the

King of the Déise for the island, which the king gave to him.

When Declan returned to his new island; his followers were afraid

of being cut off from the mainland if there was bad weather and the lack of

room. Declan asked God to push back the sea, so they could have more

land. The sea began to go back Declan ordered his disciples to follow him

to their new land. As the sea parted, a young boy called Mainchin became

scared of what was happening and told God that he had done enough.

Upon hearing this, the sea stopped, and Declan wasn't happy. He struck

Mainchin on the nose causing three drops of blood to fall, Declan quickly healed the nose and the three drops of blood created a holy well.

By this time, Patrick had arrived in Ireland and had begun his mission and met the four Bishops. Patrick told them of his mission, but Ibar initially refused to accept Patrick as the patron of Ireland because he was a foreigner. Declan having befriended Patrick earlier, welcomed him to Ireland and convinced the others to welcome Patrick. Patrick made Ailbe, the Patrick of Munster and Declan the Patrick of the Déise. Declan and Patrick's friendship would endure, even saving the Déise from being cursed by Patrick who was fooled by the King of Cashel.

Declan was known for performing many miracles, including healing people, saving Cashel from a plague and even raising the dead on a couple of occasions. Declan travelled to land of his ancestors in Meath where he was given land by the King of Tara to set up a monastery. This would explain why a number of places in Meath, especially near Ashbourne are named after Saint Declan. He had many followers with Saint Macliag being the most prominent. Saint Macliag was believed to be related to Declan, either a nephew or cousin and had a monastery at Kilmacleague, near

Tramore in County Waterford. Some believe that Declan might have named Tramore as well.

In his final days, Declan moved from his monastery to a small hut, a mile from Ardmore, so he could study and work in peace. Knowing his time was near, he returned to Ardmore and called for Saint Macliag to give me his last rites. Saint Declan died on 24th July which is his feast day. Saint Declan is still remembered fondly today. There are still buildings all over County Waterford named after him, such as Saint Declan's National School in Waterford City. His feast day is still celebrated, in Ardmore there is a Pattern Festival which happens for a week around his feast day. In 2013 the path he walked from Ardmore to Cashel was restored and opened to the public.

Ardmore: Declan's City

Ardmore Round tower, Oratory and Cathedral

Situated on the South West coast of County Waterford, Ardmore is a small village known for its history. Founded by Saint Declan, the most

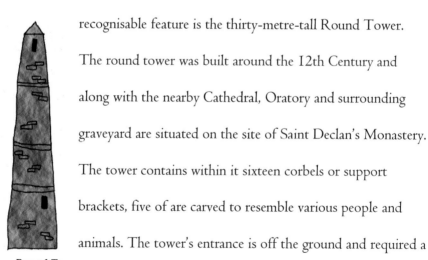

Round Tower

recognisable feature is the thirty-metre-tall Round Tower. The round tower was built around the 12th Century and along with the nearby Cathedral, Oratory and surrounding graveyard are situated on the site of Saint Declan's Monastery. The tower contains within it sixteen corbels or support brackets, five of are carved to resemble various people and animals. The tower's entrance is off the ground and required a ladder to access, one of the ledges near the door still has the grooves where the ladder was used.

St. Declan's Cathedral

Not far from the round tower is Saint Declan's Cathedral. The

cathedral was finished before 1203 A.D. as the grave of Bishop Eugene

stated that he died after he had finished the cathedral. Parts of the cathedral

date from the 9th Century all the way up to the 12th Century and it is

possible that the cathedral was built on the remains of an older church.

The cathedral is best known for its Western Wall which has several images from the bible carved into it.

Cathedral's West Wall

The images are:

Left Arch

o   Left Niche: An Equestrian figure

o   Centre Niche: Adam and Eve with the Tree of Life and the

Serpent

o   Right Niche: The conversion of the Pagan Prince of the

Déise

Right Arch

West Wall Right Arch

o   Top: The Judgement of King Solomon

o   Bottom: The Nativity with an animal on a pedestal with

Mary and the baby Jesus and the Magi bringing their gifts.

West Wall's 13 Niches

There are also 13 Niches above the arches with one or two figures in each niche. Who they are is unknown as many of the cravings have faded or seem to be missing. Some believe it could be Jesus and his disciples but there seems to be too many people depicted. Other believe the figures could be Saint Declan and his followers and the founding and Christianising of Ardmore.

Saint Declan's Oratory or the Beannachan is the one of the oldest

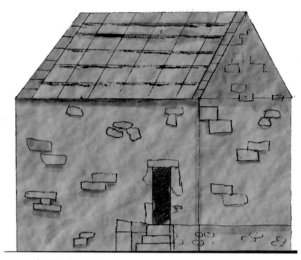

known buildings in Ardmore. Some of the lower stones date from the 8th Century. The original entrance situated in the Western Wall is now

St. Declan's Oratory

largely covered soil from the graveyard but was 1.7 metres high and 0.7 metres across. The small building has a hollow in the South-Eastern corner which is believed to be Saint Declan's grave. The soil from the grave was believed to have healing properties and according to local stories, in the 19th Century an old woman lived in the grave and sold the sacred clay to pilgrims.

Approximately 1.5 km from the round tower is Díseart Declan or

Declan's Hermitage which is where Saint Declan spent his last days. The

Hermitage

contains Saint

Declan's Holy

Well which could

have been used by

Saint Declan for

baptisms. Above

St. Declan's Well

the well there were three stone crosses showing the Crucifixion though one

cross is now missing, either stolen or it broke off and fell off the cliff into

the sea below. The Hermitage also has the remains of an early church which

during Saint Declan's Pattern, pilgrims would bless themselves with the holy

water of the well, say the Lord's Prayer and the Hail Mary, before working

three times around the church saying the Rosary. They would then trace a

sign of the cross on the cross at the Eastern Wall of the church. Children

could also be involved by being carried by their parents and tracing the sign

of the cross at the Eastern Wall.

Saint Declan's Stone which lies on the Beach in Ardmore is said to be the Stone which Saint Declan's bell travelled on and led Saint Declan to

St. Declan's Stone

Ardmore. It is believed that crawling through the narrow gap under the rock will cure you of arthritis and rheumatism. However, if you were full of sin and tried to crawl under the stone, it would collapse on top of that person, trapping them. Some believe that the stone is just a boulder from the Comeraghs brought to Ardmore by a glacier during the Ice Age. According to local folklore, a priest who regarded the practice of crawling under the stone as superstitious, got a workman to destroy the stone with a hammer. On arrival, the worker handed the priest the hammer and said; "You strike the first blow Father, and I'll finish the job." The priest refused, and the stone was saved.

Sadly, there is no sign of Saint Declan's bell, his most famous artefact. It could have been stolen or maybe hidden for safe keeping. Similarly, there is no sign of Saint Declan's remains, according to local folklore, the skull of Saint Declan was in a bad state and a local blacksmith was asked to forge several silver bands to prevent the skull from collapsing. Unfortunately, while trying to fit the bands, the skull collapsed, and the blacksmith throw away the remains and replaced the skull with a different skull.

Monks and Monasteries in the Déise

While probably the earliest Christian site in the land of the Déise, Ardmore wasn't the only one. Declan's disciple, Saint Macliag set up his monastery at Kilmacleague, near Tramore in County Waterford, so Christians in the east of the Déise didn't have to travel all the way to Ardmore to study and worship. Very little remains of Saint Macliag's monastery today apart from the decaying ruins of a church that was built on the site.

The most famous monastery after Ardmore in the Déise was Lismore. Lismore was founded in 635 A.D. by Saint Mochuda also known as Saint Carthage after he was driven out of Rathin, near Tullamore in County Offaly. The saint arrived in the land of the Déise and was welcomed by the King of the Déise. The King allowed the saint to build to a Lios on a site that the saint had spotted while traveling to see the King. While he and his followers were building their enclosure, a local woman approached them and asked them what they were doing. They replied; "We are building a small lios", to which the woman looking at their work replied; "This is not a small lios (Lios beg) but a great lios (Lios Mór)."

Saint Mochuda only lived two years after his monastery was built but Lismore still thrived and quickly became one of early Christianity's most important and famous centres for worship and study. Lismore Castle stands on the site of the original monastery, but the monastery did leave two important artefacts. The first is the Lismore Crozier, a staff used by bishops which is said to contain the oak crozier used by Saint Mochuda himself. The second artefact is the Book of Lismore, a medieval book, which contains the history of various saints. Both artefacts were found hidden in 1814 A.D. hidden in a blocked passageway while the castle was being renovated.

Monasteries generally followed a similar design to Ringforts, they

were circular enclosures with a ditch and fence and had several buildings

within, made from

waddle and daub

or stone. The

buildings in a

monastery

included the

church which were

of simple design. A

kitchen and

A Monastery

refectory where the monks prepared and ate their meals. The library and

scriptorium for storing and creating religious and historical texts. A

workshop and forge for making tools and equipment. The monks lived in

separate cells, with the abbot's cell being separate from the others. Farm

buildings were kept outside the monastery.

The monastery also had at least one high cross and a graveyard. The

graveyard was reserved for saints, monks and locals and would sometimes

have the grave of a famous religious person. Outsiders could only be buried in a monastic graveyard if the monastery believed they were worthy.

Naturally everyone wanted to be buried in one of the big monastic

graveyard like Ardmore and Lismore.

The monks wore white tunics with a hooded cape made from undyed wool and only wore sandals when working or travelling. Their hair was shaved on the top and front but allowed to grow long at the back. Their days were not just about worshipping, they copied and created manuscripts, and helped with the day to day

A Monk

running of the monastery, such as doing farm work and forging equipment.

The early churches were rectangular buildings and followed a template designed by Saint Patrick. They were ranged from 4.5 metres to 18 metres in length and had an east to west orientation with the door on the western side. They were made of either oak or stone, with sometimes very tall and pointed roofs. The doors and windows were wider at the bottom and narrower at the top. The interiors were very simple, with

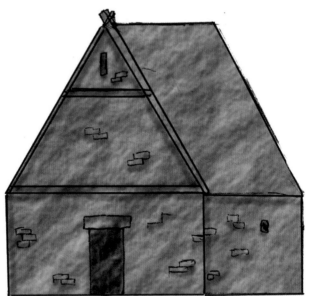

Early Church

little decoration and having no distinguishable chancel, the area around the altar which is reserved for the choir and clergy. Some churches had a boundary made of either standing stones or trees; generally oak or yew; which marked the land owned by the church. Anyone who entered this boundary could claim sanctuary, this meant that no-one could do them harm as long as they remained within the boundary. They couldn't stay forever and would have to leave when the immediate threat to them had passed.

For the everyday person the transition to the Paganism to Christianity was made as painless as possible. Churches were built near Pagan sites to entice new converts and not change the religious routine of the public. The Brehon Laws were largely kept intact which only a small number of laws which went against Christian Doctrine either changed or removed. Christian festivals were based on existing Pagan festivals, the festival of Imbolc used by the Pagans to celebrate the coming of Spring became the feast day of Saint Brigid.

In time, many Irish monasteries and churches would become famous around the known world with people travelling to places like Ardmore and Lismore to become more learned Christians. Of course, the Déise travelled overseas themselves for knowledge, trade and conquest.

Chapter 5: The Welsh Connection

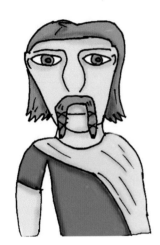

Eochaid

As seen from the Expulsion of the Déise, the Déise weren't afraid of travelling long distances to achieve their goal. By approximately 270 A.D. the Déise led by Brecc, Eochaid, Forad and Óengus had arrived in Ard Ladrann on their journey to find a new home. While Brecc, Forad and Óengus would stay in Ard Ladrann until being forced out leading to the Déise travel to the Kingdom of Osraige and then into Munster; Eochaid decided to travel with his family across the Irish Sea to Wales to find a new home. This led to Eochaid being known as Eochaid Allmuir, of Eochaid Over-Sea

Wales was part of the Roman Empire; which at this time was in the middle of a great crisis. Constant civil wars and changes in leadership, meant that the Roman Britain was vulnerable to constant attacks. By 270 A.D. Roman Britain was being attacked from the North by the Scots and Picts, Saxons and Franks in the South and the Irish in the West. Instability in Mainland Europe along with attacks from the Saxons and Franks led to the creation of a line of fortifications along the English Channel called the Saxon Shore.

With the constant attacks from invaders, it is hard to imagine how the locals reacted to the arrival of Eochaid and his family. Given that they were just trying to find a new home, it is unlikely they were greeted with too much hostility. Eochaid and his family arrived in the Welsh Kingdom of Demetia on the South-West coast, which encompassed present day Pembrokeshire and parts of Carmarthenshire. Very little is known about the Déise's early days in Wales; they seem to have integrated well into Roman Society taking on Roman-Welsh names and eventually marrying into the local populace. At the same time, they brought with them and held on to a lot of their Irish traditions and customs. Eventually Ogham Stones along with the Irish language and literature started to spread around South-West Wales.

By 382 A.D, Britain was still under Roman Rule, with Magnus

Maximus being the commander of

Britain. Magnus would become

Emperor of the Western Roman

Empire in 383 A.D. until 388 A.D.

Though the Empire would survive

until 476 A.D, there were signs of the

Empire weakening as invasions and

Magnus Maximus

raids by Barbarians were becoming more

frequent. In 367 A.D. raids from Picts, Irish, and Saxons happened

continuously for a whole year and while the raids were eventually stopped, it

showed that the Roman Empire was more vulnerable than ever.

With Irish raids becoming more frequent in the West to get slaves

and other resources, Magnus decided to improve the area's defences as he

had done in other parts of the country. He had to ways of doing this, the

first was to move entire tribes to the vulnerable areas or he gave the main

tribe in the area greater authority. Due to this policy, a lot of areas of

Roman Britain were ruled by local tribes rather than a central Roman

authority especially after Magnus left in 383 A.D. with a large portion of the Roman army to make his bid to become Emperor. As part of his new policy, Magnus made a deal with Aed Brosc, Eochaid Allmuir's grandson, to take control of Demetia and ironically protect it from Irish Invaders which may have included people from the Déise.

Having been in Wales for three generations and the Déise had become a very respected tribe in Wales. They had become integrated with the Welsh nobility through various marriages. With the new authority given to them by Magnus, the Déise became even more powerful and influential. Aed Brosc's son, Triffyn Farfog married Gweldyr, the sole heiress of Demetia and took on the Roman Name Valerian. This showed that the Déise had been romanised and had become part of the Roman ruling elite. Valerian through his marriage became the first Irish King of Demetia.

With the Déise now the part of the ruling elite some of their

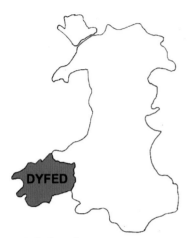

influences started to show, Demetia would eventually be renamed Dyfed based on the old Irish pronunciation for Demetia. Around Wales, places dedicated to Irish saints such as Patrick and Brigid began to appear. It also seems that the Déise in Wales kept in

Dyfed's Location

touch with their Waterford cousins as places dedicated to Saint David,

Patron saint of Wales, appear in County Waterford, such as Saint David's

Well near Clashmore. As mentioned in a previous chapter, there are

mentions of Saint Declan and Saint David meeting each other, but it seems

unlikely at this time, as Declan is supposed to have lived in the 5th Century

and David in the 6th Century.

By 436 A.D. raids by the Irish were now getting worse and the

Romans were generally relying on mercenaries to strengthen their army.

However, these mercenaries weren't easily to control and constantly asked

for more money and provisions. Aurelius Ambrosius decided to adapt

Magnus Maximus's plan by making various self-sufficient and trustworthy tribe in charge of that region's Roman army. The Déise were one such tribe and therefore became the commanders of the Roman army in Dyfed.

The Roman Empire fell in 476 A.D but the Kingdom of Dyfed remained as did the Déise legacy. One ruler called Vortipor who ruled in the 6th Century is mentioned in the Expulsion of the Déise as Gartbuir mac Alchoil as a direct descendant of Aed Brosc. Despite this, there is very little information about his reign or even his existence. An interesting stone was discovered with his name on it but that may not even be the case as we will see later in this chapter.

The kingdom of Dyfed merged with the Kingdom of Brycheiniog around 650 A.D, this merging would last for roughly a hundred years. In 810 A.D. the last direct male descendant of Aed Brosc, Owain ap Meredydd died. Whether there were any female descendants is unknown. In 904 A.D, Dyfed was conquered by Cadell ap Rhodri of Seisyllwg and later under his son Hywel Dda ap Cadell, Wales was united.

The Evidence

The evidence for the Déise being in Wales isn't definitive at this time. So far, the only major written account of the Déise being in Wales in The Expulsion of the Déise, which as we know may not be accurate. The lack of definitive written source is compounded by the Welsh's own history with some ancient Welsh scholars accepting the Déise lineage and other scholars accepting the idea that the Dyfed lineage came from Saint Helena.

Another area of contention is the scale of the Déise in Wales, was the whole tribe of Eochaid Allmuir that was relocated to Dyfed or were the tribe already there when Magnus asked for their help and they simply married into the existing ruling dynasty. Similarly, when they arrived is also up for contention, the Expulsion of the Déise suggests that the Déise arrived in Wales around 270 A.D, which others believe it must be closer to around the time of Magnus.

Despite the conjecture and confusion, there is still evidence of the Déise in Wales. Wales has the largest number of Ogham stones outside of Ireland with approximately thirty-five definite Ogham stones recorded.

Furthermore, the majority of these stones are found in Dyfed and Brycheiniog with Dyfed having roughly twenty of these stones.

One of the most interesting is the Vortipor Stone currently housed in the Carmarthenshire Museum. The stone has a Latin inscription, "MEMORIA VOTEPORIGIS PROTICTORIS" or "The memorial of Voteporix the Protector" on the face of it, but the stone also has an ogham inscription on the left-hand side. The ogham

The Vortipor Stone

inscription says "VOTECORIGAS". The fact that the two inscriptions don't match is a topic of debate with scholars, of course there is no 'P' in the Ogham alphabet. Similarly, whether the stone is referring to Vortipor, the High King of the Dyfed is also up for debate.

Conquest and Commerce

The Déise as with the rest of Ireland didn't just isolate themselves from the rest of the world. Instead they traded with visitors and travelled to other countries to acquire valuable commodities. The fact that many ancient

scholars had knowledge of Ireland without visiting the Island, clearly

showed that Ireland was visited by sailors, mostly like from Phoenicia.

Ptolemy was known to get his information from visiting Phoenicians

leading to one of the most detailed maps of Ireland in ancient times.

As well as the Slige network discussed in Chapter 2 and the

numerous tracks that could be travelled, given that Ireland is an island,

travelling by boat would be a critical way to travel. The main type of boat

used was called a currach or naomhógs as they called by the Déise and in

other parts of South Munster. Naomhógs were generally longer than other

currachs around the country at the time, but the design was generally the

same. A naomhóg

was a long wooden-

ribbed boat with a

A Naomhóg

mast and sail and were covered in either wooden planks or animal hide,

depending on the availability of wood.

Despite their relatively simple design, they were proven to be very

reliable and seaworthy. Various Romans mention seeing naomhógs whenever the Irish raided Britain, and it has been reported that one King had around fifty naomhógs travelling between Ireland and Scotland. Saint Brendan used a naomhóg when undergoing his famous voyage. Smaller naomhógs were designed to be as light as possible to allow people to carry them on their backs when travelling overland, so they could better traverse rivers and lakes. As well as people using their own naomhógs, river ferries were also used as the Brehon Laws listed a number of strict regulations. Of course, as with today boats were not just used for business, they were used for pleasure as well and again the Brehon Laws listed how compensation should be given, if a boat was damaged while being used for pleasure.

When travelling overseas, the Déise were interested in acquiring materials and knowledge. As with anyone, items of luxury such as gold and silver items, rare and precious stones, fabrics and weapons were high on the trading or raiding agenda. Knowledge was also sought, with the sharing of ideas and knowledge being very common especially amongst the learned classes. Saint Declan was known to make various trips to Mainland Europe and Wales to further his knowledge. Of course, people from overseas visited Ireland to acquire goods and knowledge. For foreign traders; jewellery, wood, animal skins and wool along with food were very popular items to acquire in Ireland. Many scholars travelled to places like Lismore, Ardmore and Clonmacnoise to further their studies. There was also a large fair and market held every three years in Carman, County Kildare part of the market being dedicated for foreign merchants to sell their goods.

Another thing that the Déise sought out were slaves, which were either bought or taken from foreign lands. Probably the most famous person to be taken as a slave would be Saint Patrick, who was taken from his home by Irish raiders and forced to become a slave. The number of slaves that could be taken at a time is staggering, Saint Patrick mentions he was just one of a thousand slaves taken during that one raid. Slaves were part of Daor Aicme class; known as daer fuidhirs and therefore had very few rights. Generally, slaves were given land which  *A Slave* was hard to farm due to being inaccessible or just being of poor quality. Their owner could also allow them to farm good land if he or she wished, but no matter what the land, they could charge as much rent as they want. The Brehon Laws also tried to limit the number of slaves anyone one tribe could have and stated that the work performed by any slaves had to be of benefit for the entire tribe, sadly these was rarely enforced. The Brehon Laws did state that unless a slave was a criminal, their owner was responsible for their slaves' well-being.

Slaves could in time become members of the tribe, as they were allowed to progress in society. If a slave made a deal with their owner and that deal was honoured by both sides, then the slave would gain some status. Over time this status and wealth would grow and could only be stopped if the slave broke the law. In most incidents, a slave's family could have some connection with the tribe by the third generation and eventually they would be allowed to marry into the tribe and with that family's original status of being slaves would be forgotten.

As the Déise travelled around Europe, they left their mark wherever they travelled. Irish literature began to appear in oversea monasteries, certain languages began to use Irish words and especially around the British Isles, large standing stones inscribed with an Irish alphabet appear across the land. These stone were Ogham stones.

Chapter 6: Ogham, The written language of the Deise

Scattered around the land of the Déise and beyond are standing stones with a mysterious series of lines carved along one side. This series of lines formed the earliest written Irish language; Ogham. There are over three

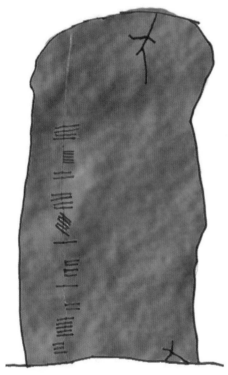

An Ogham Stone

hundred recorded Ogham Stones in Ireland with the south of Ireland having the largest amount with County Kerry believed to having over one hundred and thirty. County Waterford has the third largest amount with around fifty recorded Ogham stones. Outside of Ireland, Wales has the largest number of Ogham Stones with around forty.

The origin of the language is unknown with many myths and theories having emerged over the years. The first myth deals with Fénius Farsaid, a descendant of the Biblical Magog, who travelled to the remains of the Tower of Babel to study the various languages spoken there. By the time he and his followers arrived, the speakers of the languages had already dispersed. Fénius and his followers stayed at the remains of the tower to create the "Bérla tóbaide" or the "selected language" merging all the best parts from all the languages. He then created Ogham to be the written version of his language.

Ogma

The second myth focuses on Ogma of the Tuatha Dé Danann. Ogma was the God of speech, language, eloquence and learning. According to the myth, Ogma created the language for the learned. The first message was a warning to Lugh written on a birch containing seven 'B's making some believe that the letter B is named after the Birch tree and the other letters are also named after trees.

Apart from the myths, there are two main theories surrounding the origin of Ogham. The first theory states that with the threat of invasion always a possibility especially from the Romans, the Irish created their own language, one which couldn't be understood by anyone using Latin. This also lends weight to the theory that; since Ogham was apparently created for the learned class and the Ogham letters may have been names after trees which were believed to be mystical; Ogham could have been used by the Druids to communicate in secret.

Even after some of the Déise travelled to Wales, they still used Ogham to possibly keep messages secret. Though the fact that many Welsh Ogham stones are bilingual, suggests that maybe in time, using Ogham as a secret language fell out of favour, especially as the Déise became more powerful in Wales.

The second theory is that Ogham was created by early Irish Christians. The theory states that the Christians needed a way to write short messages in Irish. However, translating Irish into Latin was difficult, so a third language was created. This would explain why a lot of Ogham stones seem to have very short inscriptions, but many scholars believe that Ogham was created by Pagans and therefore predates Christianity. Ogham could have just been created as a written language for Irish to help with communication. Of course, the true origin is a mystery and probably will be for years to come.

The fact that Ogham stones have short inscriptions has made many wonder what the purpose of the language was and how much it was used in day-to-day life. This is due to lack of any other written evidence of Ogham barring the stones. So far, there are no books or manuscripts from the time of the Déise written in Ogham. We know from various Irish myths and legends that Ogham was written on rods of wood and served a similar purpose to letters.

This does suggest that Ogham could have been on a regular basis and the fact that these letters were written on wood, could mean that over time they rotted away or were destroyed. The same goes for books and manuscripts, they could have been destroyed or lost. Various stories about Saint Patrick and other saints, do mention the Pagan Irish and Druids had books but none of the stories describe what written language was used in these books. Similarly writing in Ogham seems to have largely phased out around the 6th or 7th Century when writing in the Latin Alphabet became the standard for scholars around Europe. For many scholars, the idea of Ogham being used for writing books seems implausible as to many, the alphabet was too cumbersome to be used for anything but short messages.

Whether Ogham was used as a common written language or as a secretive and sacred written language will be probably be debated for years to come. What cannot be denied is the importance of Ogham. Ogham not only is the earliest form of written Irish, but it is to date the only written record left by the Irish people before the arrival of Christianity. This allows the people and tribes inscribed on them a sort of immortality, since as long as the stones and inscriptions survive, they will not be forgotten.

The Ogham Alphabet

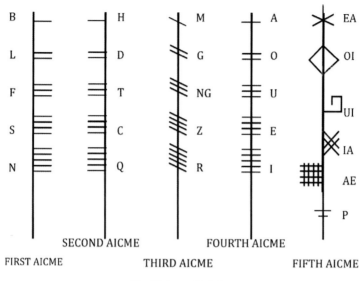

The Ogham Alphabet

The Ogham Alphabet consisted of twenty sets of parallel lines either running horizontally and diagonally and six additional symbols, all linked on a central line called the flesc. The alphabet is divided in 5 groups called aicme. The first aicme consisted of the letters 'B','L','F','S','N' and were represented by horizontal lines to the right of the flesc.

The second aicme consisted of the letters 'H','D','T','C','Q' and were represented by horizontal lines to the left of the flesc. The third aicme consisted of the letters 'M','G','NG','Z','R' and were represented by diagonal lines running through the flesc. The fourth aicme consisted of the vowels 'A','O','U','E','I' and were represented by horizontal lines running through the flesc. Vowels were sometimes represented as dots on the flesc instead of lines.

The final aicme was a later addition added to allow Ogham to be used in manuscripts and was called the Forfeda. Unlike the others the Forfeda used symbols instead of parallel lines a barring the addition of the letter 'P' consisted of pairing of letters including: 'EA', 'OI', 'UI', 'IA', 'AE or X'.

Ogham is read from the bottom up or if written horizontally, from right to left, with the first aicme pointing below the flesc and the second aicme pointing above the flesc.

The Purpose of Ogham Stones

While across the British Isles there are over four hundred known Ogham stones, the exact purpose of these stones is still unknown. This is due to large number of these stones haven't withstood the test of time. They have been damaged due to nature or negligence and some have been defaced when the stone was repurposed. One of the biggest problems in understanding the purpose of these mysterious stones is that some of them have been moved from their original location and therefore the context of the stone and the location is lost. The lack of any ancient written records about the purpose of the language itself also provides a barrier to understanding these stones.

Despite these barriers, there are some clues to the purpose of these stones. Nearly all the stones have a name, some also mention either the person's father or tribe or both. This suggests that these ogham stones could be headstones or even memorials. It has also been suggested given that some Ogham stones seem to be in areas where there were no obvious signs of burial, that they could been used as boundary stones, with the person inscribed on the stone being the landowner. Both theories are plausible, of course it is hard to say for certain especially if the stone has been moved. Maybe one day the true purpose of these mighty stones will be revealed.

The Locations of Ogham Stones

As mentioned, Ogham stones are scattered across the British Isles, with the majority of them located in Counties Kerry, Cork and Waterford. The largest collection of Ogham stones is in the Stone Corridor of University College Cork's Main Quadrangle Building. This collection is made up of stones that were moved by various 19th Century antique collectors. While the stones have been moved from their original locations, they are well preserved.

In County Kerry, which has the most Ogham stones in the world, there is an interesting Ogham Stone circle as near the Gap of Dunloe. The circle consists of eight Ogham stones, seven are believed to have come from a nearby souterrain, while the eight was taken from a ruined church. According to local folklore the stones circle was created around 1945, though for what reason is unknown.

In the land of Déise, there are a number of interesting examples.

The first is the Ogham stones at Drumlohan, near Kilmacthomas. These stones were discovered in 1867,

Drumlohan Ogham Stones

when a local farmer discovered a souterrain which had ogham stones built into the walls and ceiling. In the 1930's some of the Ogham stones were removed and placed standing next to the souterrain.

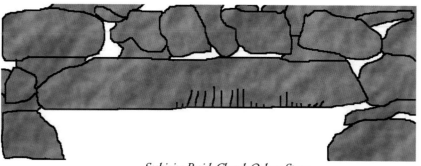

Seskinian Parish Church Ogham Stone

Seskinan Parish Church in Knockboy, County Waterford, is noteworthy for having seven Ogham stones, six of them were used as lintels and parts of archways in the church while the seventh is standing freely. St Declan's Cathedral in Ardmore, County Waterford has two Ogham stones.

One is in a small niche within the Cathedral, while the other is lying near a grave.

In the garden of Comeragh Lodge, Kilcomeragh, County Waterford, there is an Ogham stone. According to local folklore, the owner of the lodge, Mr. Palliser was travelling around Rathgormuck, when he saw some workmen trying to convert the Ogham stone into a gatepost. Realising what they were doing, he offered to build them a proper gatepost in exchange for the stone, which he moved.

In Wales, most of Ogham Stones can be found scattered around Dyfed. The Segranus Stone dubbed the Rosetta Stone of Ogham by locals, is founded inside Saint Thomas's Church in Saint Dogmaels. The stone has both Latin and Ogham inscription and was used by locals to translate Ogham.

The most famous Welsh Ogham stone is the Vortipor Stone currently housed in the Carmarthenshire Museum in Abergwili. This is another stone with Ogham and Latin inscriptions and may be a memorial to Vortipor, the High King of the Dyfed who apparently ruled in the 6th

Century. However, this stone is heavily debated by scholars due to the lack of evidence that Vortipor even existing and that the two inscriptions do not match.

Ogham Today

The Ogham alphabet may have fallen out of favour with the learned class in the 6th or 7th Century but it still exists to this day. It is still being used on headstones and is very popular on jewellery. In roughly the last forty years, Ogham jewellery has become more and more popular with necklaces, bracelets and wedding rings,

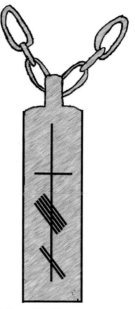

Ogham Necklace

having Ogham inscriptions. This allows Ogham to remain in the hearts and minds of Irish people and hopefully will continue to remain there for generations to come.

Chapter 7: Demise of the Déise

After finally finding their home in Munster, the Déise thrived in their land and slowly managed to become one of the most important tribes in Munster. Part of this was due to the Déise having two monastic cities at Ardmore and Lismore which attracted people from all over Europe. Despite of or because of this success, the Déise had to be wary of threats all around them.

One of the constant threats to the Déise was attacks from other tribes and kingdoms. The Kingdom of Ossory was probably the biggest threat, with both Kingdoms trying to overwhelm the other. At one point, the Déise managed to reach as far as Gowran, Co. Kilkenny before being pushed back across the Suir, when the Ossorians launched a series of counterattacks.

In 812 A.D, the Vikings arrived in the Déise and raided Little Island, where Waterford Castle is located. The Vikings would continue their attacks until 902 A.D, when they were largely driven out of Ireland. At first the Vikings just raided the land, but in time the Vikings would settle.

The Vikings returned in 914 A.D with a large fleet and landed at Waterford. It is believed that the Déise and the Vikings came to an agreement which led to the creation of Waterford City. It is possible that the Vikings just conquered and defended their new lands, especially as in 916 A.D, there were "floods and countless sea-vomitings of ships and boats" according to one writer. The Déise and the Vikings would in time become strong allies, eventually marrying each other and defending their land from Brian Boru and later the Normans.

By 981 A.D, Brian Boru was expanding his Kingdom and becoming the most powerful man in Munster. Daniel O'Faoláin, the King of the Déise wasn't pleased with Brian's expansion and attacked some of Brian's men and stole approximately three hundred cattle. Brian furious at this outrage, marched on Waterford and ravaged the City. In time the city was rebuilt and the Déise and the Vikings became allies of Brian by the time of the Battle of Clontarf in 1014 A.D. At the Battle of Clontarf, the Déise and the Waterford Vikings were led by Mothla O'Faoláin who was made commander of Brian's middle charge. Though Brian's army was victorious,

he along with a number of his generals including Mothla were killed.

Murray O'Bric kills two O'Faoláins and is later burned

As stated in a previous chapter, the Déise were ruled by two families, the O'Faoláins who ruled as the king and their cousins the O'Brics were ruled as the prince. In 1031 A.D, the two families started a vicious feud which would last nearly one hundred years. The feud seems to have started at a battle near Sliabh gCua in West Waterford where, two of Mothla O'Faoláin's brothers were killed by Murray O'Bric. It would be nearly twenty years before the O'Faoláins would get their revenge by capturing and burning Murray.

The O'Faoláins didn't stop there though. They hunted Murray's brother, Malachy O'Bric who took refuge in a souterrain. Unable to follow him into the souterrain, Malachy O'Faoláin ordered his men to set the souterrain's entrance on fire and suffocated Malachy O'Bric. In 1067 A.D, Malachy O'Faoláin fought a battle against the O'Briens, who had now become the most powerful family in Munster. Malachy O'Faoláin was captured and the O'Briens handed him over to the O'Brics who gouged out his eyes. Gouging out a prisoner's eye or eyes was common practice, especially if the prisoner was of royalty, since the law stated that a person must be free of blemishes to rule. By gouging out the eyes, it would leave a permanent blemish and prevent that person from ever ruling. Despite this,

Malachy O'Faoláin would continue to rule the Déise for another eighteen

years

Malachy O'Faoláin ordering the souterrain to be set on fire

and later a prisoner of the O'Bric's

The feud lasted until 1153 A.D when the last of the O'Brics was captured and killed by the MacCarthy family. The feud was over, but the constant in-fighting had weakened the Déise. Compounding the Déise's weakened position was they had to defend their Kingdom from other Kingdoms. In 1050 A.D, Diarmait mac Máel na mBó, the King of Leinster attacked and burned Waterford City in an attempt to take the City. The city was attacked again in 1088 A.D by the people of Dublin leading to the deaths of many Danes. In 1137 A.D, Dermot MacMurrough tried to take the city as part of his attempt to become High King of Ireland. While he failed to take the city, it was badly damaged due to fire. This constant fighting with other tribes and each other would leave the Déise and the Irish in general, vulnerable against the Normans.

The Norman Invasion

In 1167, Dermot MacMurrough was ousted as the King of Leinster by Ruaidrí Ua Conchobair, the High King of Ireland after he had abducted

Dervorgilla, the wife of the King of Breifne, a kingdom situated where Counties Sligo, Leitrim and Cavan are today. Some sources such as the Song of Dermot and the Earl suggest that the abduction was pre-planned and that Dermot and Dervorgilla were lovers, many sources though suggest that the abduction was nothing more than an abduction.

Dermot MacMurrough

Enraged at losing his Kingdom, Dermot travelled to England where he pleaded his case to King Henry II. Henry wasn't interested in Irish politics and was busy dealing with problems within his own Kingdom to intervene. Instead, he allowed Dermot to recruit anyone from within his Kingdom to aid him. Amongst the Norman Nobles recruited where Raymond FitzGerald also known as Raymond Le Gros and Richard de Clare better known as Strongbow.

Richard de Clare aka Strongbow

Strongbow had fallen out of favour with Henry after he had sided with King Stephen against Henry's family during a civil war which lasted from 1135 and 1153 A.D. When Henry became King in 1154 A.D he punished his family's enemies like Strongbow by taking away their land and titles. Realising this, Dermot enticed Strongbow, by promising his daughter Aoife in marriage and Strongbow would inherit his Kingdom after he died.

In 1169 A.D, the first Normans army led by Robert FitzStephen, landed at Bannow, County Wexford. The Normans marched on Wexford town and quickly took it. Dermot and his new Norman allies proceeded to reclaim his capital at Ferns before retaking the rest of Dermot's former kingdom.

Norman Knight

The Normans quick victories were due to their superior weapons and tactics. A Norman Knight was armed with long swords, lances, crossbows, long bows, halberds and maces and were protected by chain mail armour and helmets. The Irish were armed with battle-axes, shorts swords, spears, slings, and were protected by linen tunics and the glibb hairstyle. When it came to tactics the Normans had previously defeated the Welsh and the Irish used similar battle tactics as the Welsh, so the Normans had experience. The Irish tactics were generally quite crude, largely involving mass charges with little

Déise Soldier

strategy. The constant fighting with each other, also meant that Irish tribes were unlikely to help each, if one was under attack, resulting in weakened fractured tribes against a united professional army.

In May 1170 A.D. Raymond FitzGerald landed in Baginbun, south of Fethard-on-Sea in County Wexford. He was quickly joined by Hervey de Montmorency and the two Normans created a promontory fort in preparation for Strongbow's arrival. The fort was soon attacked by a combined force of the Déise, Waterford Danes and various local tribes, 3,000 men strong. Raymond had only eighty men, ten men-at-arms and seventy archers and

Raymond FitzGerald

it is believed Hervey probably had a similar number. Outnumbered over ten-to-one, the Normans had to rely on their fort's defences, superior weapons and tactics to survive. To gain the upper hand, the Normans released all the animals from the fort towards the attackers. The ensuring chaos allowed the Normans to gain the advantage and defeat the attackers, resulting in one thousand Irish and Danes killed and seventy of Waterford's most influential people captured.

On 23rd August 1170 A.D, Strongbow landed in Ireland at Crooke in County Waterford with twelve hundred men including knights, archers and men-at-arms. Raymond FitzGerald travelled from Baginbun with his troops to meet him and the two marched on Waterford City. While Waterford City wasn't part of his new Kingdom, it was a strategically important city. Waterford controlled the waterways which led from Wales into Leinster and Waterford acted as a gateway between Leinster and Munster. As Waterford was a key port used by many people travelling to and from Wales. The Normans could easily get information about the city. Maurice de Prendergast, a Norman noble was sent by Strongbow to Ossory and had taken part in the Siege of Wexford, travelled through Waterford on his way back to Wales and gave Strongbow a good description of the City and its surroundings.

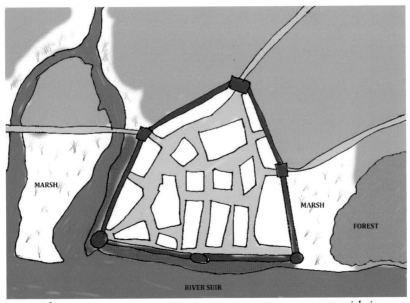

Along *Waterford City around the time of the Siege* with its

mighty walls and towers, Waterford was well defended by natural barriers

such as the Suir and slobland by the waterfront. From the Mall to Newtown

was mostly bog and marsh, this meant the Normans had to travel from

Crooke, near Passage East to the areas around the south and west of the city

to attack it. The Déise led by Melaghlin O'Faoláin rushed to the aid of their

Danish allies who were led by Sitric with Ragnald MacGillemory to defend

the city. On 25th August 1170 A.D, the Siege of Waterford began around

the area now known as Arundel Square.

Despite planning to take a walled city, the Normans were not equipped with catapults or mangonels, though some reports suggest they may have built them on site rather than transporting them. Instead they relied on scaling ladders to attack the city. Despite the Normans having superior weapons and armour, the Deise/Dane forces had the advantage. The defenders used large rocks which could be pushed from the walls on top of the attackers. Also due to the use of scaling ladders, the effectiveness of the Normans' long lance and bows were negated. Similarly, the Norman's cavalry was useless in a siege. The defenders' weapons were better suited to close range combat, allowing weapons like the defender's battle-axe to be used to devastating effect, able to penetrate and crush the Normans' armour. The Normans were forced to rely on halberds and maces.

The Normans were forced to retreat and regroup. Time after time they attempted breach the cities defences, but they were repelled. During one retreat, Raymond FitzGerald noticed a potential weakness in the city's defences. A building either sentry tower or a house was built overhanging part of the wall with a wooden frame supporting it. The Normans pulled down at the wooden frame which caused part of the wall to collapse. The Normans poured through the breach and now able to use all their weaponry effectively. They were ordered to kill anyone who was armed and resisted

leading to the deaths of over 700 people including Sitric and city fell.

Melaghlin O'Faoláin, his son and Ragnald MacGillemory were captured

and sentenced to death, but Dermot MacMurrough, who had travelled from

Ferns with Aoife for her wedding to Strongbow, managed to convince his

son-in-law to spare their lives. Strongbow and Aoife were soon married, and

the Normans now controlled Waterford.

In 1171 A.D, the political landscape of the Déise and Ireland

would change forever. In May Dermot MacMurrough died and Strongbow

proclaimed himself King of Leinster through his marriage to Aoife, which

was a legitimate claim under English law. The Irish rejected his claim as

under the Brehon Laws, women couldn't claim kingship, nor could kingship

be claimed through a woman. Instead the Irish saw Dermot's son, Domhnall

as King of Leinster, while the Normans saw Domhnall as a usurper. This

conflict between the two legal systems would continue until the 17th

Century.

By this time, Henry II was getting concerned with the rate of

Strongbow's successes. With Strongbow now King of Leinster and in control of both Dublin and Waterford, two of the country's largest ports,

King Henry II

Henry was fearful that Strongbow and the other Norman Nobles were planning to create their own independent Norman State. To this end, Henry refused to give them any more supplies. To appease Henry, Strongbow sent Raymond FitzGerald and other nobles to assure the King that they were loyal to Henry and their invasion was done so Henry could rule Ireland. Strongbow also promised him control of Waterford, Dublin and some other strongholds to prove he was loyal to the King. Henry accepted Strongbow's offer and decided to visit Ireland.

As he travelled towards Waterford, a Lord attempted to stop the King' fleet by placing chains across the river. However, he was quickly caught, and the chains removed. Henry arrived in Passage East on 17th October 1171 with five hundred knights and approximately four thousand archers and men-at-arms. Unlike Strongbow, Henry's troops were equipped with siege engines if they needed them. Henry entered Waterford the next day where he was received by the City's inhabitants who were amazed by the wealth of supplies the King had brought with him. The Déise and other Irish tribes welcomed the King and swore loyalty to him, mostly in attempted that it would stop the Normans invading their kingdoms. The Norman Nobles also reaffirmed their loyalty, especially after Robert FitzStephen had been captured by the Irish was given to Henry as a "gift" and was imprisoned in Reginald's Tower. Robert's imprisonment was mostly done by Henry to secure the goodwill of the Irish and to set an example to the Normans.

Henry remained in Ireland until April 1172 A.D where he left Robert FitzBerard in charge of the City. Henry was determined to ensure loyalty in his new Irish kingdom, so he made sure that the people left in charge were not associated with the initial invasion. The peace between the Normans and the locals was an uneasy one. Despite having sworn loyalty to Henry, the Irish were constantly wary of the Normans breaking their word and invading their lands. It didn't take too longer for the peace to be broken as many of the Norman Nobles began to invade more of the country.

In 1173 A.D. the Garrison in Waterford were becoming rebellious due to lack of pay. Raymond FitzGerald returned to the City has the new commander of the troops. To satisfy his men, he raided Lismore and the surrounding area. While they were transporting their loot back to Waterford, they were attacked by a combined force of Danes from the sea and the Irish by land led by Dermot MacCarthy. Despite this, Raymond and his forces were victorious and managed to get their loot back to Waterford. It seems that shortly after this, that Raymond asked Strongbow for his sister; Basilia, in marriage. Strongbow refused, offending Raymond who left Ireland for Wales.

In 1173-1174 A.D, Henry II faced a civil war when his eldest son, Henry along with some of his brothers and nobles rebelled. Needing as many Soldiers as possible to defend his throne, he recalled the garrisons of many towns and cities to strengthen his army. This included the garrisons of areas like Waterford. This recall of troops couldn't have come at a worse time for the Normans in Ireland. In 1174 A.D, Strongbow was defeated near Thurles by Dónal Mór O'Brien, the King of Limerick and Strongbow retreated to Waterford. Unfortunately for him, news of his defeat had reached the city and other Norman occupied areas before him and with most of the City's garrison gone, the Déise and the Danes rebelled and retook the city.

The Norman nobility along with their allies was trapped in Reginald's Tower while Strongbow and his forces were forced to seek refuge at Little Island, where Waterford Castle is situated. Strongbow had to ask Raymond FitzGerald for help and give in to Raymond's earlier demands for Basilia. By this time, Henry II had managed to secure his throne and turned his attention to the rebellion in Ireland. Raymond was now able to gather a force of four hundred and fifty soldiers and arrived in Ireland. Raymond quickly relived Strongbow and retook Waterford, just as the Danes were planning a final attack on Reginald's Tower. Soon the rebellion was crushed around the country. The Danes were seen by the Normans as the masterminds of the rebellion and were severely punished. They lost all their status and the Normans no longer trusted them. They were expelled from Waterford City and settled in what is now Ballytruckle named after Turgesius/Torcal, the Viking Chief that Turgesius Tower was also named after.

It is at this point, that Henry II proclaimed the "Laudabiliter", a Papal Bull issued by Pope Adrian IV, which gave Henry permission to invade Ireland to bring the Irish Church more in-line with the rest of the Catholic Church and bring about social and political reform. The Laudabiliter was first proclaimed in Waterford in 1173 A.D and has become one of the most controversial documents in Irish history.

The controversy with the Laudabiliter arises from the fact no-one is sure at this time if it even existed. According to records, it was issued in 1155 A.D, but it was only proclaimed in 1173 A.D, nearly twenty years later. Some believe that Henry wanted to act on the Laudabiliter earlier but his mother, the Empress Matilda convinced him not to. Despite Henry having the Laudabiliter, he never mentioned it to his forces when Dermot MacMurrough was recruiting them back in 1167 A.D. Similarly, Henry never mentioned the Bull while he was Ireland for nearly six months, even though he met with the clergy in both Lismore and Cashel. As Henry was in trouble with the Vatican following the murder of Thomas Becket in 1170 A.D, telling people he had Papal backing at the time, might have damaged his claim instead of strengthening it. It should be noted that the Laudabiliter was proclaimed after Henry had reconciled with the Pope.

Also, the Laudabiliter gave Henry permission to invade in order to bring reforms but Henry's reason for going to Ireland in 1171 A.D was a pre-emptive move against the Norman Nobles in Ireland rather than anything to do with the Irish.

As well as Henry not mentioning the Laudabiliter, to date there is no physical evidence of the actual document or even a copy in ether the Vatican or English archives. Matters to do with Ireland don't seem to appear in the Vatican archives until 1215 A.D. The lack of the evidence in the Vatican is compounded by the fact that in letters between Henry and both Popes Adrian IV and Alexander III, the Laudabiliter wasn't mentioned. The first written record of the Laudabiliter and what it contained comes from Giraldus Cambrensis or Gerald of Wales in his book Expugnatio Hibernica in 1189 A.D. Whether the Laudabiliter was real or not, wasn't a concern at the time, it helped cement the Norman's power in Ireland and was even used by the Irish, in later years when appealing to various Kings about the condition of Ireland.

In October 1175 A.D. Henry signed the Treaty of Windsor with Rory O'Connor, High King of Ireland and Connacht to secure peace between the Irish and the Normans. The treaty allowed Rory to remain as High King if he recognised Henry as his King and paid him a tribute. Any Irish that had been displaced by the Invasion could peacefully return to their lands and any Irish King could retain their land by paying a tribute to Rory. The treaty quickly failed to maintain the peace as neither King had the power to stop their subjects.

Rory as King of Connacht had little influence on the Irish in Munster and other areas, which led to the Irish making raids on Norman areas. Henry at this time was more concerned with his Kingdom in France so the Normans could expand their territories without the consent of Rory or Henry and with no fear of being punished. In the land of the Déise, under the treaty, the lands between Waterford and Dungarvan were put under Norman rule despite those lands not being conquered by the Normans. Two years later the Normans expanded their rule beyond Lismore, creating County Waterford. The Déise responded by making raids on various Norman areas.

In 1177 A.D, Henry made Robert le Poer, marshal of the land from Waterford to the River Blackwater near Lismore. This appointment removed whatever power the O'Faoláin's had in the eyes of the Normans. Robert didn't have much time to enjoy his new lands as he died in 1178 A.D, his family, the Powers, would remain a powerful and influential family for many years. Strongbow died in 1176 A.D from blood poisoning, while Raymond FitzGerald died sometime after 1185 A.D, and buried in Molana Abbey near Youghal, while Henry II died in 1189 A.D.

The people who caused the Demise of the Déise were dead, but the legacy of their actions would affect Waterford and the island of Ireland for centuries. As for the Déise, their power was gone but they would not be forgotten.

Chapter 8: Up the Déise! The Déise's Legacy

Following the Norman Invasion, the Déise's power and influence seemed to be gone, but that wasn't true. As with Strongbow and his claim to the Kingdom of Leinster in 1171 A.D. in the eyes of the Normans and English, the Irish laws and customs had no relevance anymore. However, for the native Irish, since the invaders had illegitimately taken power, the Normans laws and customs had no power over them. This meant that in the eyes of the Irish, the O'Faoláins were still Kings of the Déise and rulers of their lands, not the Normans. This legal duality would last until the 17th Century.

In 1181 A.D, the Déise attacked and plundered Lismore as revenge for the Normans taking their land. When Prince John as Lord of Ireland, arrived in Waterford in 1185 A.D, the O'Faoláins as Kings of the Déise, were one of the many Irish rulers to welcome the Prince. But many of the Prince's men having never seen an Irishman before, began to ridicule the Irish's appearance. Whether the Prince himself was involved in debatable, though he angered

Prince John

the Irish further by giving their lands, which some had managed to retain due to having a good relationship with the Normans, to his friends and followers. The Déise and other Irish tribes rebelled against the Prince. John's actions led to the Normans losing territory and even made enemies with the Norman Lords by giving the tax revenue which was supposed to go towards defending their lands to his friends who squandered it on luxury items and parties. The crisis was averted when Henry II learned of what was going on, recalled his son and followers back to England and sent John de

Courcy to quell the Irish. It was during this visit that Prince John built Lismore Castle.

Irish chronicles such as the Annals of Four Masters continue to mention the O'Faoláins as the Kings of the Déise in the early 13th Century. They mention that Art Corb O'Faoláin was King of the Déise when he died in 1203 A.D and was succeeded by Daniel O'Faoláin. Disaster struck the Déise in 1204 A.D when a plague ravished the land and according the Annals, emptied most of the houses in the Déise. Daniel O'Faoláin was killed in 1206 A.D in Cork with Meyler Fitz Henry's army.

In 1096 A.D, the Diocese of Waterford was created, leading to a divide in the religious order in the Déise. The Bishop of Lismore had previously been in charge of all religious matters in the Déise and now it was being split between two Bishops. Tensions rose as the Bishops of Waterford were Normans, while the Bishops of Lismore were Irish.

In 1204 A.D, David was appointed Bishop of Waterford, and he wasn't very popular with the Irish, the various Irish chronicles refer to David as the 'foreign bishop' indicating their hatred of him. David was a cousin of

Meyler Fitz Henry the Justiciar or Chief-Governor of Ireland and a friend of King John, who as we know wasn't popular with the Déise. John also gave David land around Dungarvan. In 1207 A.D, Bishop David attacked Lismore and began to seize land from Malachias, the Bishop of Lismore. David claimed that Malachias had been excommunicated and therefore it was his right as the only serving Bishop to seize Lismore for the sake of the church. Bishop Malachias asked Pope Innocent III for help and had proof that the letters that showed he had been excommunicated were fake. The Pope ordered Bishop David to stop and submit to the orders of the Pope and appear before a council of three Irish bishops to settle the matter. Bishop David never appeared before the council as he had been killed.

The King of the Déise an O'Faoláin had tried to get the two Bishops to compromise but was unsuccessful, partly due to the Déise King's own hatred towards Bishop David. The matter came to a brutal end when a member of the O'Faoláin family murdered Bishop David. Whether he was murdered by O'Faoláin himself or one of Princes is unknown as sources differ. What happened to this O'Faoláin is unknown as this was the last mention of the Déise in the Annals. Unfortunately for the Déise and the Bishop of Lismore, David's successor Bishop Robert II was even more troublesome, going so far as attempting to arrest Bishop Malachias in order to seize Lismore. Bishop Robert II and his conspirators were eventually excommunicated for their actions. The tensions between the Diocese of Waterford and the Diocese of Lismore would continue until the two Dioceses were merged in 1363 A.D.

Throughout the years, various members of the Irish Nobility attempted to create hereditary titles associated with the Déise. Maurice Fitzgerald, Baron of Dromana, created the title of Viscount Decies on 31st January 1569 A.D. Unfortunately, the title became extinct when he died on 28th December 1572 A.D without a male heir. On 9th October 1673 A.D, Richard Power, a descendant of Robert Le Poer, 1st Earl of Tyrone, 6th Baron Power of Curraghmore, and Governor of Waterford, recreated the title Viscount Decies. Richard died in 1690 A.D and his eldest son, John inherited his father's titles becoming the 2nd Viscount Decies. John had no children, so when he died in 1693 A.D, his titles were passed to his brother, James.

James became the 3rd Viscount Decies but when he died on 19th August 1704 A.D without a male heir. His daughter Catherine couldn't inherit her father's titles as they were created to be inherited by male heirs.

This meant that all of James's titles including his viscountcy became extinct

and no-one has created the title of Viscount Decies since. Catherine married

Marcus Beresford in 1717 A.D, who recreated the Earl of Tyrone title had

used to belong to Catherine's father. Catherine and Marcus had nine

children, their youngest son, William Beresford would become Bishop of

Ossory and Archbishop of Tuam and created the title of Baron Decies, of

Decies, co. Waterford on 22nd December 1812 A.D.

When William died in September 1819 A.D, his eldest son John

Horsley-Beresford became the 2nd Baron Decies. This title has continued

throughout generations of Beresfords with Marcus Hugh Tristram de la

Poer Beresford being the 7th Baron Decies.

In 1002 A.D, King Brian Boru became High King of Ireland and

declared that all surnames should be fixed, to ensure that people could tell if

they descended from a principal family or not. Despite the clan being called

the Déise, the surname Deise, Desie or Dease was retained in County Meath

by the Déise who remained in Meath and weren't expelled by Cormac Mac

Airt. For instance, Thomas Dease was Bishop of Meath from 1621 to 1652 A.D.

The surname Deasy also comes from the Déise, but whether it is from the North or South Déise is unknown as the name can be found in Counties Cork and Mayo. It is possible that the Deasys came from the South Déise and settled in Mayo and took the name Deasy is honour of where they came from. According to one family legend, the Cork Deasys come from the survivor of a massacre in Waterford and was protected by the O'Donovan family.

For the Southern Déise, the surnames of O'Faoláin, O'Bric and O'Eachtraig were used, referring to the tribe's main families. The O'Bric surname, anglicised as Bric or Brickley is found in Kerry, Galway and South Tipperary, though in Waterford, they are still remembered as one of the City's most famous locations is name after them, BallyBricken which means Town of the Brics. O'Faoláin was anglicised as either Phealan or Whealan while O'Eachtraig was anglicised as either Hearne or Ahearne, these surnames are still prominent in Waterford City and County.

The Decies spelling of Déise has been used by in the naming of two Baronies in County Waterford, "Decies without Drum," and "Decies within Drum". "Decies without Drum" consisted of much of the lands between Kilmacthomas and Cappaquinn, including Dungarvan. "Decies within Drum" consisted of the lands south-west of Dungarvan, including Helvick and Ardmore. The name comes from the Drum Hills, which cross part of County Waterford.

Waterford Hurler

Decies is also the name of the journal published by the Waterford Archaeological & Historical Society. Similarly, there are many businesses and organisations in Waterford City and County that have the word Déise in their name. These range from charities to DIY stores, fan clubs to sport shops

Of course, when the county teams play a hurling or Gaelic football match, banners and the cry of "Up the Déise!" can be heard all around the county of Waterford. Proving the Déise are gone but not forgotten.

Aed Brosc (c340 A.D -?) Grandson of Eochaid Allmuir and leader of the Déise in Wales. He made a deal with Magnus Maximus which saw the Déise becoming protectors of Demetia. His children would rule the Kingdoms of Demetia/Dyfed and Brycheiniog.

Aoife MacMurrough: (c1145 A.D – c1188 A.D) Daughter of Dermot MacMurrough and Wife of Strongbow. Her marriage to Strongbow allowed him to become King of Leinster under English law but not Irish law. She was buried in the crypt of Kilkenny Castle. Her daughter Isabel de Clare's descendants would include a large number of British Royals and Nobles.

Art Corb O'Faoláin: (? – 1203 A.D) King of the Déise. Not much is known about him except he died in 1203 A.D and was succeeded by his son Daniel.

Bishop David the Welshman: (? – 1209 A.D) Bishop of Waterford from 1204 A.D -1209 A.D. A friend of King John, he was very unpopular with the Irish. He seized land from the Bishop of Lismore and even ignored the Pope's orders to stop. He was murdered by a member of the O'Faoláin family.

Bishop Malachias: (? - c1216 A.D) Bishop of Lismore from 1203 A.D -1216 A.D. In 1207 A.D his diocese was attacked by Bishop David the Welshman in an attempt to increase his own power base. He asked Pope Innocent III for help, but David refused to obey. The matter was "resolved" when David was murdered in 1209 A.D.

Brecc: (3rd Century A.D) One of four brothers who led the Déise during their expulsion. His sons were later tempted to return to Tara but Óengus promised them, that they would become leaders of the Déise if they stayed.

Brian Boru: (941 A.D – 1014 A.D) High King of Ireland from 1002 A.D – 1014 A.D. Descended for the Déise who later moved to County Clare, he eventually became King of Munster before later becoming High King of Ireland. His relationship with the Déise was mixed with the

Déise either fighting for or against him. He died at the Battle of Clontarf in 1014 A.D.

Cairbre Lifecahir: (c235 A.D – c285 A.D.) Son of Cormac Mac Airt who succeeded his father as High King of Ireland. He helped his father defeat the Déise and banish them from Tara. Best known for his war against Fionn mac Cumhaill and the Fianna, which led to the group's destruction. He died in battle against Fionn's grandson, Oscar.

Cellach: (3rd Century A.D) Prince of Tara and son of Cormac Mac Airt. He abducted Forach, a Déise princess and fled to Tara seeking his father's protection. He was killed by Óengus of the Dread Spear when he refused to release Forach.

Claudius Ptolemy: (c100 A.D – c170 A.D) Greco-Roman mathematician, astronomer and geographer who was born in Alexandria, Egypt. Best known for his works the Almagest and the Geography. Ptolemy's Geography contained the first detailed map of Ireland or Iwernia as he called it, which contains rivers, tribes and towns.

Constantine (272 A.D – 337 A.D) Also known as Constantine the Great and Roman Emperor from 306 A.D – 337 A.D. He converted to Christianity and introduced tolerance to Christians leading to Christianity becoming the main religion of the Roman Empire.

Cormac Mac Airt: (? – c267 A.D) High King of Ireland who ruled for forty years. In most accounts he was portrayed as a wise king and a skilled leader, though in some accounts like the Expulsion of the Déise he was portrayed in a poor light. After losing his eye to Óengus, he retired and wrote The Book of Aicill, one of the earliest law books.

Crimthann mac Énnai (? – c483 A.D) King of Leinster who allowed the Déise to settle in Ard Ladrann in exchange for marrying a number of Déise princesses. One of his daughters was Ethne the Dread. He was killed by Eochaid Guinech his own grandson.

Dáire: (3rd Century A.D) Prince of Tara and son of Cormac Mac Airt.

Daniel O'Faoláin: (? – 1206 A.D) King of the Déise from 1203

A.D – 1206 A.D, following the death of his father Art Corb O'Faoláin.

During his reign in 1204 A.D, a terrible plague stuck his Kingdom. He was

killed in Cork with Meyler Fitz Henry's army.

Daniel O'Faoláin: (10th Century A.D) King of the Déise around

981 A.D. He attacked Brian Boru and stole approximately three hundred of

his cattle. Brian retaliated by attacking and burning Waterford City.

Dermot MacMurrough: (1110 A.D – 1171 A.D) King of Leinster

from 1126 A.D –1167 A.D. He lost his title when he abducted the wife of

the King of Breifne. He made a deal with the Normans to reclaim his

Kingdom, including promising his daughter Aoife to Richard de Clare. His

death and burial at Ferns, County Wexford led to a power-struggle between

Strongbow and Dermot's son, Domhnall.

Diodorus Siculus: (1st Century BC) Greek Historian who was born

in Agira, Sicily. Best known for his forty-book work the Bibliotheca

Historica which detailed the geography and history of the world. Ireland is

mentioned in his work as Iris, but he made some false claims about the Irish.

Eochaid: (3rd Century A.D) One of four brothers who led the Déise during their expulsion. He would later move to Wales where his family would marry into the local Roman Nobility and create a dynasty of Welsh-Irish Kings. He was given the name Eochaid Allmuir since he travelled overseas.

Ethne the Dread: (? - c490 A.D) Daughter of Crimthann mac Énnai and Congain. It was prophesied that she would lead her people to their new home. She was feed young boys to magically age her. She fulfilled her destiny when she married Óengus mac Nad Froích who gave her people land as part of her dowry.

Fiachu Bacceda: (3rd Century A.D) Ruler of a small kingdom in Leinster who aided the Déise against the Uí Bairrche and gave the Déise their lands.

Fionn mac Cumhaill: (3rd Century A.D) Irish hero and leader of the Fianna who had many epic adventures around Ireland. The adventures of Fionn and the Fianna were believed to have taken place during Cormac Mac Airt's reign.

Forach: (3rd Century A.D) Déise princess who was kidnapped by Cellach, son of Cormac Mac Airt. She was rescued by her family and her mistreatment at the hands of Cellach caused the Déise to rebel and later be banished from Tara.

Forad: (3rd Century A.D) One of four brothers who led the Déise during their expulsion. He was the eldest brother but was not the leader as his mother was a slave. His sons were later tempted to return to Tara but Óengus promised them, that they would become leaders of the Déise if they stayed.

Gaius Julius Caesar: (100 B.C – 44 B.C) Roman politician and general, who conquered large parts of Western Europe. Set up the idea of a Roman state ruled by one man. He wrote a first-hand account of his conquests in the Gallic Wars, where he mentions Ireland or Hibernia as he called it.

Gallienus (c218 A.D – 268 A.D) Roman Emperor from 253 A.D until 268 A.D. He ruled during what was known as the Crisis of the Third Century. Though he was a capable leader, he couldn't prevent various Roman providences splitting from Rome. It was during his reign that the Expulsion of the Déise is supposed to have happened.

Geoffrey Keating/ Seathrún Céitinn: (1569 A.D – 1644 A.D) Irish Historian from County Tipperary who wrote in Irish. His book Foras Feasa ar Éirinn/ Foundation of Knowledge on Ireland described Ireland's history up to the Norman Conquest. He was one of many Irish historians who tried to disprove the claim of ancient scholars about the Irish.

Giraldus Cambrensis: (1146 A.D – 1223 A.D) Also known as Gerald of Wales, he was known for his extensive travels. His books Topographia Hibernica and Expugnatio Hibernica detailed the Irish way of life and the Norman Conquest of Ireland.

King Henry II: (1133 A.D -1189 A.D) King of England from 1154 A.D – 1189 A.D. Grandson of Henry I, he became King in 1154 A.D following the death of King Steven. He gave his blessing to the

Invasion of Ireland, but later had to take matters into his own hands, when

he feared Strongbow was going to create his own state. He was succeeded by

his son Richard I also known as Richard the Lionheart.

King John: (1166 A.D – 1216 A.D) King of England from 1199

A.D – 1216 A.D. Son of King Henry II he was made Lord of Ireland by his

father in 1177 A.D and became King of England following the death of his

brother Richard the Lionheart. His first trip to Ireland in 1185 A.D was

seen as a disaster and John was best known as one of the main villains in the

Robin Hood stories.

Magnus Maximus: (c335 A.D – 388 A.D) Roman General,

Commander of Britain and Western Roman Emperor from 383 A.D – 388

A.D. To secure Britain's borders from raiders, he would settle tribes in

vulnerable areas and give those tribes more authority. One tribe that

benefited from this strategy was the Déise in Wales.

Malachy O'Faoláin: (? – c1085 A.D) King of the Déise during the

O'Faoláin/O'Bric feud, he was responsible for the death of Malachy O'Bric

by suffocating him when his men set fire to the entrance of the souterrain

O'Bric was hiding in. He was captured by the O'Brien family in 1067 A.D and was given to the O'Brics who gouged out his eyes. Despite this, he led the Déise until around 1085 A.D

Maurice Fitzgerald: (1530 A.D – 1572 A.D) Baron of Dromana and 1st Viscount Decies, a title he created in January 1569 A.D. He married was Ellen FitzGerald. They had no children, so his titles became extinct.

Melaghlin O'Faoláin: (11th Century A.D) King of the Déise during the Norman Conquest. He led his men during the Siege of Waterford in 1170 A.D. Following the City's defeat, he was captured and sentenced to death, but his life was spared by Dermot MacMurrough.

Meyler Fitz Henry: (? – 1220 A.D) Lord Chief Justice of Ireland from 1200 A.D - 1208 A.D. The son of one of King Henry I's illegitimate son, he was related to many Norman Nobles including King Henry II. He took part in the Norman Conquest where he was known for his bravery and was part of the Waterford Garrison during the revolt in 1174 A.D. As Lord

Chief Justice of Ireland, he dealt with matters involving the King, which usually led to him battle both the Irish and Norman Nobles.

Mothla O'Faoláin: (? – 1014 A.D) King of the Déise at the time of the Battle of Clontarf in 1014 A.D. He was part of Brian Boru's army and oversaw Brian's middle charge. He was killed in the battle and two of his brothers were later killed at the start of the O'Faoláin/O'Bric feud.

Óengus mac Nad Froích (c430 A.D - c 490 A.D) King of Munster who following the death of his wife, tried to woo Ethne the Dread. He granted her three wishes if she agreed to marry him. He was the first Christian King of Munster and was later killed with his wife at the battle of Cenn Losnada.

Óengus: (3rd Century A.D) Leader of the Déise and wielder of the Lúin Celtchair, the Spear of Lugh. Also known as Óengus of the Dread Spear and it was claimed he had the strength of fifty men. It was Óengus who lead the Déise against Cormac Mac Airt which led to Cormac's blinding. Óengus later gave up his family's claim to the Déise leadership to prevent his nephews from returning to Tara.

Pope Adrian IV: (c1100 A.D – 1159 A.D) Pope from 1154 A.D until 1159 A.D. His name was Nicholas Breakspeare and to date the only British Pope. He supposedly issued the Laudabiliter in 1155 A.D, which gave Henry II permission to invade Ireland in order to reform the Irish church.

Raymond FitzGerald: (12th Century) Also known as Raymond Le Gros (The Fat), he was one of the Norman Nobles who assisted Dermot MacMurrough in retaking his kingdom. He served as Richard de Clare's second in command during the Norman Invasion. He died sometime between 1186 A.D and 1198 A.D and was buried in Molana Abbey.

Richard de Clare: (1130 A.D – 1176 A.D) Probably better known as Strongbow, he was the 2nd Earl of Pembroke and aided Dermot MacMurrough in retaking the Kingdom of Leinster. He was commander of the Norman Forces and managed to capture Waterford where he married Dermot's daughter Aoife. He died of blood poisoning and was buried in Christ Church Cathedral, Dublin.

Richard Power: (1630 A.D – 1690 A.D) Governor of Waterford in 1661 A.D and 6th Baron le Power and Coroghmore, County Waterford. He created 1st Earl of Tyrone and recreated the extinct title of Viscount Decies on the same day in October 1672. He was part of the Jacobite army during the Williamite War from1688 A.D until 1691 A.D. He was captured during the Siege of Cork in 1690 A.D and died in the Tower of London. His titles were passed to his sons John and James, but the titles became extinct when both died without male heirs.

Robert le Poer: (? - 1178 A.D) Marshall of Waterford from 1177 A.D – 1178 A.D. He was one of the many knights that arrived with King Henry II. His descendants, the Power family would remain a powerful and influential family for many years.

Rory O'Connor: (c1116 A.D - 1198 A.D) King of Connaught from 1156 A.D to 1186 A.D and High King of Ireland from 1166 A.D – 1198 A.D. He was the last High King of Ireland before the Norman Invasion. He signed the Treaty of Windsor in1175 A.D with Henry II to try and ensure peace between the Irish and the Normans but was unable to prevent both sides from attacking the other.

Saint Ailbe (? – 528 A.D) Patron Saint of Munster. He was seen as the "leader" of the four pre-Patrick saints in the south of Ireland, which included himself, Saint Declan, Saint Ibar and Saint Ciarán. He founded the monastic centre at Emily in County Tipperary and was buried in Cashel. His feast day is 12th September.

Saint Ciarán: (5th Century A.D) Patron Saint of Ossory and regarded as the first Saint to have been born in Ireland. He was one of four Saints working in Ireland before Saint Patrick. Also known as Saint Ciarán the Elder to avoid confusion with the founder of Clonmacnoise. His feast day is 5th March.

Saint David: (c500 A.D – c589 A.D) Patron Saint of Wales. Some claim that he and Saint Declan encountered each other but the dates make this almost impossible. Despite this, he was seen as a link between the Déise in Ireland and Déise in Wales as seen from Saint David's Well near Clashmore. His feast day is 1st March.

Saint Declan (5th Century A.D) Patron Saint of the Déise. He was responsible for converting the Déise to Christianity. He founded Ardmore and was buried in Saint Declan's Oratory or the Beannachan. He was one of four Saints working in Ireland before Saint Patrick. His feast day is 24th July.

Saint Ibar: (? – 500 A.D.) Patron Saint of Wexford. He was responsible for converting the people of Wexford to Christianity and was one of four Saints working in Ireland before Saint Patrick. St Iberius Church in Wexford Town was named after him and it was where he had an oratory. His feast day is 23rd April.

Saint Macliag: (5th Century A.D) Disciple and a possible relative of Saint Declan, who had a monastery at Kilmacleague, near Tramore in County Waterford. He gave Saint Declan his last rites.

Saint Mochuda: (? – 639 A.D) Also known as Saint Carthage, he is the Patron Saint of Lismore. He was expelled from Rathin, near Tullamore in County Offaly and arrived in the Déise where he was given permission to build a new monastery. His feast day is 15th May.

Saint Palladius (? – 457/461 A.D) French Bishop who was sent to Ireland by Pope Celestine in 431 A.D to become the First Bishop of Ireland. He landed in Arklow, Co. Wicklow and attempted to convert more of the Irish to Christianity. He was later banished by the King of Leinster and settled in Scotland.

Saint Patrick: (387 A.D – 461/493 A.D) Patron Saint of Ireland. He was brought to Ireland as a slave before escaping only to return later to convert the Irish to Christianity. On his way to Rome he befriended Saint Declan. He died in Saul, County Down and was buried in Down Cathedral. His feast day is 17th March.

Strabo: (64 B.C – 24 A.D) Greek geographer, philosopher, and historian from Asia Minor, modern Turkey. Best known for his work Geographica which was divided into seventeen books. The fourth book described Ireland or Ierne as he called it, along with Gaul and Britain.

Triffyn Farfog: (385 A.D – 445 A.D) also known as Valerian, he was the First Irish King of Demetia/Dyfed. The great-grandson of Eochaid

Allmuir, he married Gweldyr, the sole heiress of Demetia and became its King.

Vortipor: (c.475 A. D – 540 A.D) also known as Gwrthefyr, he was King of Dyfed. He was in constant battles with Maelgwn Gwynedd, King of Gwynedd who tried to invade his Kingdom. The Vortipor Stone in Wales is believed to be a memorial for him and has both Latin and Ogham writing.

William Beresford: (1743 A.D – 1819 A.D) Great-Grandson of Richard Power, his mother was Catherine Power, Richard Power's Granddaughter. He was bishop of Ossory in 1782 A.D and later Archbishop of Tuam in 1794 A.D. He created the title of Baron Decies, of Decies, co. Waterford in December 1812 A.D. When he died his title was passed to his eldest son John Horsley-Beresford and the title still exists to this day.

Bibliography

Breathnach, Eamon. *History, lore & legend through the eyes of the young.* The Friendly Press, 1987.

Casey, Thomas. "The Origin and Early History of the Deisi" *Old Waterford Society Vol 2 (March 1971)* pg. 74-78.

Edwards, Ruth Dudley and Bridget Hourican. *An atlas of Irish history.* Routledge, 2005.

Egan, P.M. *Egan's Guide to Waterford,* 1894.

Ginnell, Laurence. *The Brehon Laws: A Legal Handbook.* 1894.

Guy & Co. Ltd. *Guy's South of Ireland Pictorial guide: describing and illustrating its picturesque and beautiful scenery, antiquities, &etc.* Guy & Co. Ltd., 1893.

Hansard, Joseph. *The history, topography and antiquities (natural and ecclesiastical), with biographical sketches of the nobility, gentry and ancient families, and notices of eminent men, &c. of the County and City of Waterford; including the towns, parishes, villages, manors and seats,* 1870.

Jennett, Sean (Ed.). *The Traveller's Guides: Ireland: Munster: Cork, Kerry, Clare, Limerick Tipperary and Waterford.* 1966.

Joyce, P. W. *A smaller social history of ancient Ireland; treating of the Government, military system and law; religion, learning and art; trades, industries and commerce; manners, customs and domestic life, of the ancient Irish people.* 1906.

Keohan, Edmond. *Illustrated history of Dungarvan.* 1924.

Lennox Barrow, George. *The Round Towers of Ireland.* The Academy Press, 1979.

Mackey, Patrick. *Reginald's Tower and the story of Waterford.* Pat Mackey Promotions for Waterford Corporation, 1989.

Moody, T. W. and F. X. Martin. *The course of Irish history.* Mercier Press in association with Radio Telefis Eireann, 2011.

Mulligan, Paul. *A short guide to Irish antiquities: sites shown on Discovery Series Ordnance Survey maps.* Wordwell, 2016.

O' Sullivan, Rev. B. "Celtic Paganism Still Survives in Decies ", *Old Waterford Society Vol I (1969 – 1970)* pg. 49-58.

Ó'Connor, Dónal. *Walking the holy ground in Ardmore & Lismore: early Irish spirituality. 4th ed.* An Sagart, 2002.

O'Curry, Eugene. *On the Manners and Customs of the Ancient Irish: Vol. III. By Eugene O'Curry. Edited with an introd., appendixes, etc., by W.K. Sullivan.* Lemma Publishing Corporation, 1971.

Olden, Michael and Andy Taylor. *The Parish of Tramore and Carbally: dedicated to the parishioners of Tramore and Carbally, past, present and future.* Olden & Taylor, 2006.

Olden, Michael G. *The faith journey of the Déise people: Diocese of Waterford and Lismore.* Michael G Olden, 2018.

O'Neill, Jack. *A Waterford miscellany.* Rectory Press, 2004.

Power, Patrick C. *A history of Dungarvan: town and district.* De Paor, 2000.

Power, Patrick C. *History of Waterford: City and County.* 1998

Power, Rev. P. *A short history of county Waterford.* Waterford News, 1933.

Roche, Richard. The Norman Invasion of Ireland. Anvil, 1995.

Ryan, Michael. *The illustrated archaeology of Ireland.* Town House and Country House, 1991.

Smith, Charles. *The ancient and present state of the county and city of Waterford: containing a natural, civil, ecclesiastical, historical, and topographical description thereof.* W. Wilson, 1774.

Taylor, Andy. *Tramore: Echoes from a seashell.* 1990.

Electronic Sources

"Celtic Kingdoms of the British Isles, Celts of Cymru" available from https://www.historyfiles.co.uk/KingListsBritain/CymruDemetia.htm Internet, The History Files, Accessed 2018.

"Life of St. Declan of Ardmore" available from https://celt.ucc.ie//published/T201020/index.html Internet CELT: The Corpus of Electronic Texts, Accessed 2018.

"The Expulsion of the Dessi" available from https://celt.ucc.ie/published/T302005/ Internet, CELT: The Corpus of Electronic Texts, Accessed 2018.

Index

Printed in Poland
by Amazon Fulfillment
Poland Sp. z o.o., Wrocław

55767015R00091